973
WEI

Weiss, Jeffrey.

The book of country living

STORAGE

2495

DATE			

© THE BAKER & TAYLOR CO.

THE BOOK OF
COUNTRY LIVING

THE BOOK OF COUNTRY LIVING

Jeffrey Weiss and Susan Osborn

HOLT, RINEHART AND WINSTON
NEW YORK

Published by Holt, Rinehart and Winston, 383 Madison Avenue, New York, New York 10017

Published simultaneously in Canada by Holt, Rinehart and Winston of Canada, Limited.

Library of Congress Cataloging in Publication Data

Weiss, Jeffrey.
  The book of country living.

  1. Country life—United States.   2. Country homes—United States—
Conservation and restoration.   I. Osborn, Susan.   II. Title.
S521.5.A2W44   973'.09734   81-47462
ISBN 0-03-059614-9   AACR2

First Edition

Printed in the United States of America
10   9   8   7   6   5   4   3   2   1

Produced by The Jeffrey Weiss Group, Inc., 133 Fifth Avenue, New York, New York 10010

Text by: Susan Osborn, Ken Druse, Jay Stevens, Mark Baker, Garin Wolf

Design by: Deborah Bracken

Consultant: Jean Read

Production: Tricia West

Offset printing and binding: W.A. Krueger Company

Color separations by: Kwik International Color, Ltd.

CONTENTS

Introduction

ountry living is simple, down-home pleasures. The bright colors and sweet smells of cooking in a country kitchen, the inimitable comfort of sitting in a sturdy rocker and basking in the heat of an old-fashioned, pot-bellied stove, the relaxing vista of green fields and wooded hillsides. The country life is calling and inviting you to experience its old-fashioned delights.

Today, we live in a world of chrome and plastics held together by artificial preservatives and high-powered hype. The crush of crowds, the pressures of the city, the failures of a disposable culture are all more than enough to drive us to the country life.

Country is not just a way of life. It's a state of mind. The country life-style harks back to a time when people knew they could depend on themselves even when they couldn't depend on anthing else. Our ancestors' lives were not nearly as simple as our nostalgic revelries would have us believe. They built their own homes and furnishings with a rough but loving craftsmanship, grew most of their own food and lived of necessity in harmony with the land and their neighbors.

The Book of Country Living will help you get acquainted with the time-honored virtues and unpretentious beauty of life in the country. And it will show you how to bring a little bit of the country to wherever it is you live, whether that is downtown Chicago, suburban Atlanta, or urban San Francisco.

It's time to get back to basics. Folks from Maine to California are restoring old houses and barns and furnishing them with the treasures of yesterday. All over America, people are taking a joyful step back in time, decorating their homes with cherished heirlooms, crafts and collectibles. And there are hundreds of reasons why.

COUNTRY IS BEAUTIFUL

The naive artistry of plain folks is apparent everywhere in a country home. The earth colors of natural dyes and paints, made from the soil itself, warm the heart. Bright reds, greens and sky blues in the calico prints of a patchwork quilt are "suitable for framing." The stenciled likeness of flowers and doves speaks of hope and love and home. There is something uniquely handsome in a simple wooden spoon, carved by hand and glowing from generations of use.

COUNTRY ENDURES

In the early days of America, when a pioneering family found a place to put down roots and set up housekeeping, they first had to build a house that might be a log cabin, a clapboard farmhouse or a general store with a living space on the second floor. No matter how humble, the house had to stay warm and dry through every kind of weather. It was a matter of survival. When a man built a bedstead, a table or a cabinet, he built it to last a lifetime. Each chair and sideboard had to be something with which he could live and of which he was proud.

We are the lucky inheritors of our ancestors' care and attention to detail. Country furnishings are made of solid materials that are reluctant to fall apart. Country is a thick bowl of salt-glazed pottery, beautiful to look at and reassuring to touch. Country is a hand-stenciled Boston rocker, as easy to sit in as it is to admire.

COUNTRY WORKS

When America was young, there was little time for frivolity or excess. The household goods a person owned had to work and work well. Furnishings were designed to be functional as well as pleasing to the eye. Add a little,Yankee ingenuity and a kitchen table also provided storage for flour, sugar and salt, and a Shaker sewing table had drawers on opposite sides to accomodate two seamstresses.

There was a simple reason so many bread boards were carefully engraved with the motto "Waste Not, Want Not." Every useful item, from

a handful of cornmeal to a scrap of lumber, was important to life in the country. Recycling wasn't a 20th century first. Today, all sorts of old, rustic objects can be adapted to our modern needs. A milk stool doesn't have to stay in the barn to be useful. Bring it in by the fire and use it as a footstool. By restoring homes and furnishings, we are actually recycling the past.

With the energy crisis far from over, the best example of country living economy and efficiency is the wood-burning stove. Dissatisfied with rising fuel bills, Americans have rediscovered that invention which was perfected by our renowned forebear, Benjamin Franklin. More and more people are using old-fashioned stoves to warm their homes, cook their food and heat their water.

They've also found that a crackling fire works other wonders like bringing people together over a pot of tea for some good conversation. Instead of gathering in silence in front of the television, families find themselves relaxing around the comforting warmth of their wood-burning stoves, talking and laughing about the day's activities.

COUNTRY IS HARMONY WITH NATURE

Country living doesn't stop inside the house. Much of the lure of the country life is the great outdoors. A real country home is in harmony with the land. Trees shade the house in summer and protect it from cold winds in the winter.

What would a country home be without fresh vegetables and a well-tended garden? An herb garden was an integral part of our ancestors' country homes, providing them with both seasonings for food and medicinal herbs used in home remedies. A productive easy-to-care-for garden is a natural arrangement of plants and flora, each carefully planted for easy maintenance. And, of course, flowers—both wild and cultivated—bring color and sweet scents to your surroundings.

Herbs are picked fresh for immediate use, or they can be dried, hanging in decorative arrangements from the ceiling beams. Vegetables are sliced raw and made into crisp salads or popped into the stew bubbling on the stove.

10

COUNTRY CAN BE CHALLENGING

Our ancestors worked with their hands and made for themselves most of the things that today we buy off the shelf. Cobblers' benches, pewter and pottery baking utensils, carpenters' awls, planes and punches were all made by hand and are collected today for their superb workmanship and simple elegance. Once you've started collecting, it won't be long before you'll want to try your hand at old-time country crafts. Country living is all about canning your own vegetables, preparing your own blackberry preserves and making your own baby bassinet. You may not become a master carpenter just because you collect tools for decoration, but you might be tempted to try a little wood-carving.

There are plenty of thoughtful souls who have revived the old crafts for us to enjoy. Our reawakened interest in country has inspired many crafts fairs where we can see potters at the wheel, glassblowers and smiths sweating over an outdoor furnace and quilters gossiping around their frames. Visit a crafts fair—you might discover a craft of special interest to you, one which is within your talents and your budget.

COUNTRY IS COMFORTABLE

The country life-style is built on friendliness and informality, the unexpected

guest who stops by for a minute and ends up staying for dinner. The focal point of any country home is the kitchen. In a country kitchen, chairs seem built to tip back against the nearest wall. Thick pine tables invite you to rest your elbows on them. The wicker settee on the front porch is the perfect place to watch the stars come out on a spring night. And if the evening brings a little chill, a body can always prop his feet on a stool before the fireplace.

A traveler can find no better place to rest his weary head after a long day on the road than in an authentic country inn. After a hearty country meal, the wayfarer can snuggle under a cozy handmade quilt and lay his head on a soft down pillow. You don't have to stay at home to keep that country comfort.

COUNTRY IS OUR HERITAGE

The country style is based on the rural traditions of the first immigrants. Modern country living is the best of those useful and appealing traditions. Country has become a way of life that is uniquely American. By restoring homes and furnishings we become a part of that tradition and perpetuate it. By learning to live in harmony with nature and our neighbors, we live our common heritage.

The Allure Of Country Decorating

Great Country Rooms

he insides of the very first Early American "homes" could hardly be called rooms. The explorers, missionaries and adventurers who discovered this country found shelter in a few weather-beaten campaign tents, while their followers built makeshift huts and lean-tos or simply slept out-of-doors exposed to the elements.

A few hardy settlers arrived next. Their number one priority was usually a fortress to protect them from the great unknown wilderness, so frighteningly different from the well-populated European countryside. They struggled to tame a small corner of that wilderness, clearing trees and boulders from the land, in preparation for planting the crops which would insure their continued survival. Little time and energy could be spared for building proper housing. For the first winter or two, our forebears made do with dug-outs and roofed pits (called cellars) or—taking their lead from the Indians—crude wigwams.

Those who did not freeze or starve to death and those who were not killed or captured by the natives found a very abundant land waiting for them. Within a short time, they began to prosper. And what is prosperity without a comfortable home in which to enjoy it?

The variety evident in the modern country style of today was established during the settlers' first years. The first Americans came to these shores from many, many countries. Their new homes were combinations of familiar ethnic traditions and the materials they found around them in the New World.

The Spanish Synthesis

When we consider the Europeans who came to America, we tend to picture the Pilgrims, English Puritans in their somber black clothes with buckles on their shoes. Actually, the Spaniards were among the very first to settle in America. Their homes provide one of the most striking examples of the synthesis of old traditions with new

materials and methods of construction.

As the conquistadores moved into the American Southwest, they brought with them a love for colorful terra-cotta roofs and floor tiles and for luxurious patios. The Moorish influence of decorative arched doorways and windows were combined with the Spaniards' own superb hand-wrought iron work. But in the desert regions of what is now New Mexico, Arizona and Southern California, they had no familiar building materials. So they adapted the Indians' sun-dried bricks to their architecture, and called the result "adobe." Adobe is the Arabic word for the mud and clay from which such unfired bricks were made. Adobe homes were flat-roofed, rectangular houses, built around a central courtyard. The Spaniards learned what the Indians had known for centuries: that adobes were natural solar homes. Thick clay walls absorbed the intense solar heat during the day and slowly released it for added warmth at night. An extended roof shaded windows and doorways like an awning and the high exterior walls protected the courtyard from the relentless wind and dust storms. Although the first adobe houses required extensive replastering after heavy thundershowers (to prevent them from literally washing away), many have survived for hundreds of years and are being lovingly restored by their present owners.

Antique furniture, braided rugs, beamed ceiling and stone walls make this living space a country museum.

A Taste of England

English settlers in the Northeast and along the Eastern Seaboard used the sturdy oak tree to build timber-frame houses much like the ones they had left behind in York, Cornwall and the outskirts of London. These were usually small, single-room dwellings dominated by a huge fireplace which was the sole source of heat. During the raw winter months, the only really warm place to sit was the "cubby seat," an indentation in the interior wall of the fireplace itself. The houses had beamed ceilings, casement windows and plaster walls which would seem almost familiar to us today.

The Britons also used a rather unusual method to construct houses called palisades. They would split logs and stand them in the ground vertically to form walls somewhat like the exterior walls of frontier forts we see in movie Westerns. These crude but ingenious structures were roofed with thatch. In 1685 the writer George Scot claimed that the New Jersey bank of the Hudson River was dominated by country houses constructed in this manner.

The Log Cabin

You are probably asking yourself, "What about the log cabin? Isn't that the original, truly American home?" We always imagine the early colonists at Jamestown cutting trees and erecting log buildings. In our cultural mythology the log cabin has become the symbol for American ingenuity, the poor but honest home where every president should grow up. But we now know that the tradi-

tional, saddle-notched, horizontally-laid, whole log house is a native tradition of the Germans and Scandinavians. They were first built in and from the vast evergreen forests of Northern Europe.

The Swedes built what may be the first log cabins in the New World at Fort Christina (now Wilmington, Delaware) in 1638. Instead of settling near the coast, the Scandinavians and Germans moved inland to what is now Pennsylvania, Illinois and Wisconsin. They were unable to carry the heavy tools needed to work hardwoods with them. The few rudimentary tools they did bring along were only suited for building houses from the easily cut and light-weight pine and fir trees which are so prevalent in the Northern Middle West. Other immigrants borrowed the basic structure of the log cabin and adapted it to their specific needs as they moved further and further into the frontier.

As German immigrants became more firmly established in Pennsylvania, they began to express their love of decorative detail. The elaborate handmade scroll- and fret-work which festooned the eaves and porches of their homes was the forerunner of the machine-made decorations of Victorian gingerbread houses and would have looked just right along the Rhine River or in the Black Forest.

The Barn

It may be that the only architecture truly "at home" in America is—of all things—the time-honored barn. This unselfconscious structure provided farmers with a sturdy solution to the problems of storing crops and of feeding and sheltering animals. The men and women who built them weren't professional designers by any means, but they seemed to know intuitively how to erect a building which was sound and functional, as well as pleasing to the eye. If there is a precedent for the Early American barn it is the great spacious European cathedrals.

A barn-raising expressed the spirit of brotherhood and democracy which was to typify this new land. Neighbors from miles around gathered to help with construction. When their work was completed, they celebrated a job well done by turning the barn into a gay dance hall, filled with fiddle music and whirling square-dancers.

At the turn of the present century, 85 of every 100 Americans still lived on a farm. Today, people are discovering the almost limitless possibilities of barns as living spaces and they are transforming barns into year-round homes. People are finding that there is something uniquely satisfying about the architecture of the basic American barn. Perhaps the 19th century novelist, Thomas Hardy, expressed it best when he wrote:

"Unlike and superior to either of those two typical remnants of medievalism (the church and the castle), the old barn embodied practices which had suffered no mutilation at the hands of time. Here, at least, the spirit of ancient builders was one with the spirit of the modern beholder. Standing before this abraded pile, the eye regarded its present usage, the mind dwelt upon its past history with a satisfying sense of functional continuity thoughout—a feeling almost of gratitude, and quite of pride, at the permanence of the idea which had heaped it up."

A Look Inside

Now that we have seen, in the mind's eye, the outside of an Early American home, let's step through the front door. Inside we will look for decorating ideas which can enhance the modern country style.

CANDLES AND FIRELIGHT

The lighting is dim. The earliest houses had small windows, because glazing was unavailable or extremely expensive. Besides, a window seemed just another hole for the cold winter wind to blow through. So most of the light is provided by the fireplace. Beyond the glow of the fire, an oil-burning lamp or a few precious candles flicker in the corners of the room. Every family made its own supply of candles from beef or mutton fat, beeswax or bayberry shrubs. Even so, candles were a luxury—the drippings and stubs were kept to be remelted when it was time to make new ones.

Few of us here in the 20th century want to pass all of our nights by candlelight, but soft, muted lighting which is subtly country—as well as energy efficient—can be evoked with the help of candles, a kerosene lamp or old-fashioned gaslight fixtures equipped with incandescent bulbs.

Antique country lighting fixtures are hard to find. Even those which are adaptable to electric wiring are too expensive for the pocketbook of the average homeowner. But good reproductions crafted in traditional motifs—such as cast-iron chandeliers, tin sconces and Tiffany lamps—are available from reputable craftsmen. Outfitted with such modern equipment as dimmers and low-watt bulbs, reproductions shed a delicate, subdued light.

The paraphernalia associated with candlelight

can itself add the country flavor to a room. Candleholders, snuffers and trays, as well as hurricane shades and tinderboxes are easy to come by. An old stoneware jug can be used as a lamp base. Topped with a shade covered with pleated calico fabric, it creates an instant country mood.

THE EXPANSE OF WALL

For the early Americans, the cheapest, most versatile and convenient method for decorating walls was paint. If they could afford something other than whitewash, dusky, natural earth colors were used, sometimes ornamented with stenciled folk designs.

In the middle of the 18th century, a craze for wallpaper erupted in the cities and continued as a decorating preference for many years. There were some drawbacks to wallpaper—it was expensive and fragile and it required an expert to hang it properly. For these reasons, wallpaper was not readily available to people in the country. But they still wanted their walls to look as smart and pretty as those in the city. If they couldn't get wallpaper, they painted their walls in imitation of it.

One popular technique, which is as easy to do today as it was in 1750, is called stippling. A natural sponge is dipped into an emulsion paint of a color contrasting to the color of the wall. Then the surface of the sponge is touched lightly to the wall leaving an abstract almost floral pattern.

During the late 18th and early 19th centuries, itinerant muralists roamed throughout New England, the Middle West and the South, painting frescoes on the walls of homes in exchange for room and board. Most of these folk artists depended on stencils for their designs, although some of the best painted freehand, decorating doors, windows, dados and cornices with colorful ornaments. Today, you can stencil your walls just as our ancestors did. It's easy. All you need is some oil paint and a fairly steady hand. But be careful in selecting contemporary stencils to work from. Try to find designs which are as fresh as their predecessors. Purists might want to consult *Curious Arts,* a step-by-step manual published in 1825 by premiere muralist Rufus Porter, which provides explicit instructions on wall painting and the use of stencils.

But walls don't have to be meticulously painted to have that country look. Floral wallpaper, rough plaster and recycled barn siding used for paneling all give a room some country flair.

ART FOR THE COMMON MAN

If the house we walked into was built in the early 1800s, there would probably be a landscape or portrait painting hanging on the wall, created by some local folk artist. No matter how naive an artist's work might be, these paintings were prized for the well-to-do air they lent their owners. Today, the work of well-known folk painters is outrageously expensive—especially landscapes because they are rarer than portraits. But while you are exploring the country, you might find the work of an as-yet-undiscovered artist whose work suits your taste and budget.

In the late 19th century, chromolithographs became more popular than paintings. Although they are not always appreciated by today's art historians, the art-hungry, democratic society of the 19th century craved these mass-produced color prints of popular oil paintings. There are still a number of them around today at affordable prices.

Many other kinds of folk art can be used to decorate in the country style. Needlework, old checkerboards, tavern signs, weathervanes and hunting decoys are beautiful accents in any room.

FLOORS AND CARPETS

The floor of our imaginary room is made of wide pine planks. Parquet and narrow hardwood strip floors did not become popular until the 1800s. Original floorboards can be sanded, sealed and stained or painted to achieve an old, country look. A well-sanded floor reveals a warm honey color that becomes every country setting. If you do choose to refinish your floors, don't scrape the character out of them. Sand off just enough of the surface to remove the dirt. If the house you own doesn't have wide-plank pine floors, but you would like to install them, many lumberyards can sell you new flooring. Some yards specialize in old floors which have been salvaged from demolished old homes.

Occasionally, the floors in Early American homes were stenciled with bold designs. These delightful floral and geometric patterns added color and vitality to a relatively stark environment. Some homeowners painted their floors in imitation of carpets and tiles. These attractive designs which were originally hand-rendered, are now available in stencils. Use them to create an informal, old-fashioned ambience in any room of the house.

Although needlepoint, Chinese, Aubusson and Persian carpets were found in Early American homes, most people could not afford them. More modest floor coverings such as hooked or braided rugs, made from scrap cloth, and canvas floor cloths were plentiful. Few originals are still around. Handcrafted rugs were subject to constant use and it is very unusual for one to have survived those years of pounding by hundreds of human feet. However, good reproductions are widely available. The natural fibers they are made from, including wool, cotton, linen, canvas and reed, will last a lifetime if they are properly cared for. You can still buy canvas-backed floor cloths. Stenciled, silk-screened or hand-painted, these are particularly alluring and perfect for the country style.

Country Furniture

But what of the furniture that occupied the first American homes? The colonists brought some furniture, a few kitchen utensils and dinnerware to this country. For example, a typical Dutch farmhouse along the Hudson River would have contained a fiddle-backed chair, a Freisland clock and an ornate "China carpett." This last item would have been much too valuable to lay on the floor. Instead it would have been used as a covering for the table. The Dutch *Kas*, or wardrobe cabinet,

row-back side chairs, blanket chests, dry sinks, rockers, settles, stools, trestle tables and wash-stands are reappearing in well-made reproductions. Many of these pieces are expensive, but the workmanship is high quality and the materials are unadulterated. For information on where to find reproduction furniture, see Directory.

———————————◆·◆———————————

How to Inspect Antiques Before You Buy

On the other hand, you may want to collect some of those original pieces still available from dealers and junkmen, from flea markets and high-class auction houses. Be careful how you spend your money. A clever reproduction can sometimes be mistaken for an original piece—and the difference in the price of the two will be extraordinary. The following list of checkpoints will help you determine whether or not you are purchasing the genuine article:

• Inspect the piece thoroughly, using a flashlight if necessary, to detect any alterations. Look for signs of recent workmanship. Replaced sections are often made from wood of a different thickness, color or grain from the original. Early American craftsmen did use a variety of woods, but the major pieces should be of the same thickness and age.

• Rough edges should have a similar feel and appearance. They will appear darkened with age, not newly cut.

• Check the hardware. You should be able to see where screws or hinges have been refitted during

alterations. Machine-made screws did not appear until the middle of the 19th century. Wooden pegs were often used instead of nails. Old pegs are more square than round and are not all the same size.

• Aged paint flakes off in chips. New paint is more pliable and will peel off.

• If you find two different saw marks (called kerfs) on one piece, you should suspect that at least some restoration has been done.

• Truly old pieces have a lingering odor—a genuine old spice box will smell of cinnamon or nutmeg, an old coffee grinder of rich cocoa beans. Use your nose. It will help you detect the new from the old.

• Time and use soften the features of an old piece of furniture. A housewife's broom might have hit the base of a low slung chair over and over again through the years, leaving it slightly marred. A dust rag will gradually smooth the outer edges of a wardrobe in a century. The back of a finial might be worn if the man of the house liked to lean his chair back against the wall. Old trunk lids will show wear around the edges and the stenciled or painted design on a chair slat will be worn from constant contact with the sitter's back. Look for wear where you would expect to find it if you been using the piece.

• Patina is that special character of old wood that develops from the natural wearing and aging process. Patina takes time to appear. The color darkens and the entire piece mellows with age. There is no commercially produced staining product which can give wood the evenness of character that time can. There is one stain, though, made from ammonia and plug tobacco which can mask a copy as an original and is very difficult to

row-back side chairs, blanket chests, dry sinks, rockers, settles, stools, trestle tables and wash-stands are reappearing in well-made reproductions. Many of these pieces are expensive, but the workmanship is high quality and the materials are unadulterated. For information on where to find reproduction furniture, see Directory.

How to Inspect Antiques Before You Buy

On the other hand, you may want to collect some of those original pieces still available from dealers and junkmen, from flea markets and high-class auction houses. Be careful how you spend your money. A clever reproduction can sometimes be mistaken for an original piece—and the difference in the price of the two will be extraordinary. The following list of checkpoints will help you determine whether or not you are purchasing the genuine article:

● Inspect the piece thoroughly, using a flashlight if necessary, to detect any alterations. Look for signs of recent workmanship. Replaced sections are often made from wood of a different thickness, color or grain from the original. Early American craftsmen did use a variety of woods, but the major pieces should be of the same thickness and age.

● Rough edges should have a similar feel and appearance. They will appear darkened with age, not newly cut.

● Check the hardware. You should be able to see where screws or hinges have been refitted during

alterations. Machine-made screws did not appear until the middle of the 19th century. Wooden pegs were often used instead of nails. Old pegs are more square than round and are not all the same size.

● Aged paint flakes off in chips. New paint is more pliable and will peel off.

● If you find two different saw marks (called kerfs) on one piece, you should suspect that at least some restoration has been done.

● Truly old pieces have a lingering odor—a genuine old spice box will smell of cinnamon or nutmeg, an old coffee grinder of rich cocoa beans. Use your nose. It will help you detect the new from the old.

● Time and use soften the features of an old piece of furniture. A housewife's broom might have hit the base of a low slung chair over and over again through the years, leaving it slightly marred. A dust rag will gradually smooth the outer edges of a wardrobe in a century. The back of a finial might be worn if the man of the house liked to lean his chair back against the wall. Old trunk lids will show wear around the edges and the stenciled or painted design on a chair slat will be worn from constant contact with the sitter's back. Look for wear where you would expect to find it if you been using the piece.

● Patina is that special character of old wood that develops from the natural wearing and aging process. Patina takes time to appear. The color darkens and the entire piece mellows with age. There is no commercially produced staining product which can give wood the evenness of character that time can. There is one stain, though, made from ammonia and plug tobacco which can mask a copy as an original and is very difficult to

would have dominated the room with its massive panels of elaborately carved heavy wood. The farmer slept in a *slaap banck* a heavy piece of furniture with doors which closed like a cupboard around the sleeper for warmth and privacy.

But for the most part, the settlers had to build their own furnishings. The early American farmer/craftsman had to be a jack of all trades, skillfully manipulating unsophisticated tools to turn out quality furniture. A householder might own an axe for chopping, a frow for slicing shingles, a maul for pounding and a couple of knives for cutting and carving. He used an adze for scraping, a gouge for shaping and a square to measure straight angles. If he was lucky, he might also own a scribing gauge, a gimlet and calipers. Few men actually owned all these tools; each one shared what he had with his neighbors.

Especially in the country, imported woods were simply unavailable, so many pieces of furniture were made entirely of the soft pine that was all around the countryside. That doesn't mean that their furniture was poorly constructed. Durability was the most sought after quality of country furniture. Many original pieces have survived for a hundred years or more and accent the homes of today's collectors.

For all its unadorned simplicity, there was a great variety in country furniture. Each piece was constructed to fit a particular need of the homeowner. An artisan built a cupboard to fit a particular corner of the house or designed a chest of drawers with four drawers because the owner would need precisely that many compartments for his clothing and possessions. So within a set of a few time-honored patterns, each piece was unique.

Again, paint was the most available method of decoration for the early Americans. Using folk mo-

tifs from their homelands they embellished their furnishings with striking decorations, beautifully if primitively rendered with a limited number of colors. Peacocks symbolized warmth and happiness. A many-pointed star represented man's spiritual struggle against evil. A heart represented hope and love. The dove meant peace.

THE BENCH

Country furniture is sophisticated only in its supreme usefulness. Always functional, many pieces served more than one purpose. Benches were the most common furnishing in the early years of colonization. They were used for seating in meeting houses, schools and workshops and also in homes. On many of these benches the seat was also a hinged lid for a storage compartment. Because houses were so drafty and lacked modern central heating, settle benches were built with wide wings to protect a person from nose to toes. These benches are as versatile today as they were then. You can use them in your contemporary home as seating or they make ideal storage boxes for towels, bed linens and tablecloths. They can also be turned into beautiful display stands for your treasured collections.

FORM AND FUNCTION

The best examples of utilitarian country furniture comes from the Shakers. In the late 18th century, Mother Ann Lee led a religious group, known as the United Society of Believers in Christ's Second Appearing, from England to the little hamlet of Watervliet, New York. There, the believers set up the first Shaker community which would eventually spread to Massachusetts, New Hampshire, Maine, Kentucky, Ohio and Indiana. These rigorously pious immigrants were master craftsmen whose furniture is characterized by its spare elegance. Dainty flanges and ornamented rims are not a part of Shaker design. If an object had no part in the work and well-being of their community, it was not needed at all. A slat-backed rocker was not just comfortable seating for the Shakers. It served as a tool as well. It was made with a

rung instead of finials at the top of the back posts. Upholstery mats could be hung from this rung for cleaning or repair. Idle hands are the Devil's workshop.

THE ROCKING CHAIR

The rocking chair is the most American of furniture. The first rockers were made by craftsmen in Boston who distinguished their product with a deceptively simple and consoling design. A good Boston rocker has a thick, sturdy seat which rolls up in the back and curls under in front. A bronze stenciled design was traditionally applied to Boston rockers after the year 1820. An older rocker is easy to spot since they usually have more sticks in the back support than rockers being made today. Look for at least seven of these sticks. There has never been a more compatible or companionable piece of furniture for any room in the house.

MASS PRODUCTION TAKES OVER

Handmade country furniture reached its peak popularity in the early 19th century. People were in love with massive, flat-surfaced, unadorned furnishings. Then, in about 1820, the first mass-produced chairs manufactured by the Hitchcock Company appeared on the market. With the advent of the mail-order catalogue at the end of the Civil War, mass-produced furniture became accessible to almost everyone. Handcrafted, homemade country furniture became a category of antiques.

In recent years, more and more cabinetmakers have been learning the art of designing, shaping, joining and finishing good old-fashioned country furniture. Using traditional methods, they are fashioning furniture with character, pieces that will stand the test of time. Canopy beds, benches, ar-

row-back side chairs, blanket chests, dry sinks, rockers, settles, stools, trestle tables and wash-stands are reappearing in well-made reproductions. Many of these pieces are expensive, but the workmanship is high quality and the materials are unadulterated. For information on where to find reproduction furniture, see Directory.

———————————————•——•——————————————

How to Inspect Antiques Before You Buy

On the other hand, you may want to collect some of those original pieces still available from dealers and junkmen, from flea markets and high-class auction houses. Be careful how you spend your money. A clever reproduction can sometimes be mistaken for an original piece—and the difference in the price of the two will be extraordinary. The following list of checkpoints will help you determine whether or not you are purchasing the genuine article:

● Inspect the piece thoroughly, using a flashlight if necessary, to detect any alterations. Look for signs of recent workmanship. Replaced sections are often made from wood of a different thickness, color or grain from the original. Early American craftsmen did use a variety of woods, but the major pieces should be of the same thickness and age.

● Rough edges should have a similar feel and appearance. They will appear darkened with age, not newly cut.

● Check the hardware. You should be able to see where screws or hinges have been refitted during

alterations. Machine-made screws did not appear until the middle of the 19th century. Wooden pegs were often used instead of nails. Old pegs are more square than round and are not all the same size.

● Aged paint flakes off in chips. New paint is more pliable and will peel off.

● If you find two different saw marks (called kerfs) on one piece, you should suspect that at least some restoration has been done.

● Truly old pieces have a lingering odor—a genuine old spice box will smell of cinnamon or nutmeg, an old coffee grinder of rich cocoa beans. Use your nose. It will help you detect the new from the old.

● Time and use soften the features of an old piece of furniture. A housewife's broom might have hit the base of a low slung chair over and over again through the years, leaving it slightly marred. A dust rag will gradually smooth the outer edges of a wardrobe in a century. The back of a finial might be worn if the man of the house liked to lean his chair back against the wall. Old trunk lids will show wear around the edges and the stenciled or painted design on a chair slat will be worn from constant contact with the sitter's back. Look for wear where you would expect to find it if you been using the piece.

● Patina is that special character of old wood that develops from the natural wearing and aging process. Patina takes time to appear. The color darkens and the entire piece mellows with age. There is no commercially produced staining product which can give wood the evenness of character that time can. There is one stain, though, made from ammonia and plug tobacco which can mask a copy as an original and is very difficult to detect. Examine each piece of furniture very carefully—even the insides of the drawers.

New Uses for Old Things

Country furniture includes not only those things we refer to as home furnishings. Farming implements, store props and various tools make for interesting "conversation pieces." Many rustic objects can be adapted from their humble origins for use in today's home. Milk stools, coffee bins, wagon or buggy seats, egg crates, confectionary tables, printers' boxes, dental cabinets, cobblers' benches, tobacco cabinets and bellows can be used for display or decoration. Anything that says country can be used to add the flavor of the past to your home.

Old baskets naturally complement any country decor. Woven in a variety of shapes and sizes, they make unique and versatile storage containers. Baskets can be used to hold shoes, yarn, laundry, firewood or plants. A line of miniature baskets along a windowsill makes an attractive indoor herb garden. A group of flat baskets hung on a wall can create a beautiful graphic design.

Boxes of all dimensions were essential storage containers for the early colonists. They contained their writing tools, knives, candles and other household items. Some boxes doubled as desks, others as bins for salt, spices and grain. You can use these old boxes to store and display books and stationery supplies. Knife boxes can be used for kitchen utensils or sewing equipment. Dough troughs can be used to hold children's toys or eggs in the kitchen.

A homeowner interested in the country style pays attention to detail. By making decorative use of things employed in the daily life of the past, any home can become a country retreat. Old household utensils made of pottery or glass are usually too fragile to be put to daily use, but they are perfect for display. An old stoneware jug makes an attractive vase for wildflowers and a fragile china water pitcher will delight the eye when it is filled with dried flowers. Even an old yarn winder can make an attention-grabbing abstract sculpture.

Good quality hardware, whether original or reproduction, can enhance the appearance of your home. Real Colonial hardware (like doorknobs and drawer handles) was made of glass, wood and porcelain as well as bronze, tin, copper and cast iron. Many contemporary craftsmen are making quality reproductions from traditional patterns. However, because of its weight and substance, hardware is not as likely to disintegrate with age. Some authentic pieces may still be found at junk shops and flea markets.

Accessories don't have to be old, though, nor do they have to be handmade to provide an old-fashioned country feeling. Practical and decorative reproductions of barometers, baskets, boxes, trays, clocks, doorstops, trivets, tinware, weathervanes, brooms, sugar cones and silhouettes can be used in any home. All these are widely available and are usually less expensive and easier to find than originals. The best compendium of reproduction accessories is *The Old House Catalogue,* published by Warner Books.

The Country Collector

Most country style decorators become collectors sooner or later. Who could resist all the curious items that one runs across searching for just the right piece? We usually end up buying much more than we can actually use to accent one home. But that's no problem. Collections fit perfectly into the country style. The early settlers in this country had no closets. Their solution to this problem was simple and direct. They built cupboards, shelves and boxes, and they put pegs in the walls to hang things from. In any case, most of their possessions were in plain sight all around the home. Cutlery, china, clothes and all kinds of odds and ends were everywhere. The Shakers even hung their chairs from peg racks when they were not in use.

Stately cupboards with their imposing size make safe and handsome display cases for your collection of hand-painted china, metal toy soldiers, redware, Delft or spatterware. Peg racks can be used to help keep the home tidy (as they originally were) or you can use them to display dried herbs in the kitchen, or a collection of scarves or jewelry in the bedroom.

Beds and Quilts

Perhaps the only piece of Early American furniture which does not adapt well to modern use is the bed. They are still available, but they are usually too small for today's comfort-conscious homeowner. Mattresses were more often than not large bags stuffed with rude straw or crackling corn husks. But the settlers did bring a bed furnishing

with them to the New World which is highly prized today—the quilt. They were three-layered coverlets decorated with geometric designs or leaf, shell and flower motifs. These quilts like everything else in the spare, compact Early American house were multi-purpose. They were used as room dividers, bed dressings, shawls, food covers and tablecloths.

During the first few decades of settlement, few new fabrics were imported and native textiles were not yet developed. So as quilts wore thin, they were patched with random bits of old clothes and other completely worn-out quilts. These became known as Crazy Quilts and they were magical creations alive with color and family heritage. After Eli Whitney patented the cotton gin in 1793,

Americans began to mass-produce inexpensive textiles, and quilting was no longer a salvage art. Popular designs began to appear, including Basket of Scraps, Churn Dash, Log Cabin, Whig Rose, Victory, Pincushion, Chained Loops, Nine Patch, Jacob's Ladder and Job's Tears.

Boldly patterned and brightly colored quilts make an immediate and artful statement when hung on a wall. They also make startlingly colorful tabletops, set under glass. Scraps from old quilts can be made into pillows or encased in Plexiglass and used as coasters.

Homespun, muslin and cotton were the fabrics most often used in country Colonial and Victorian homes. Cotton cloth dotted with floral sprigs was perhaps the most popular fabric of the 18th century. Fabric was used to cover walls before wallpaper was available. Reproductions of these patterns, including Chinoiserie Tree, Chelsea and Philadelphia Stripe, are immensely popular and widely available (there is probably one reproduction fabric for each year between 1700 and 1850) from leading manufacturers. They can be employed in today's bedrooms to make curtains, drapes and bedspreads reminiscent of an age gone by.

The Country Bedroom

The settlers' one-room houses had no bedrooms of course. Beds were either built into the wall or were free-standing in the main room. Any modern bedroom can be made country with the addition of a colorful quilt, a braided or rag rug and patchwork pillows. An old iron or wooden bedstead found at a flea market and freshened with a new mattress can make a cheery chaise lounge. A dressing table artfully cluttered with silver-handled hairbrushes and mirrors, and toilet water bottles add a delicate country touch.

Old children's furniture adds a nostalgic feel to any bedroom. It is functional and fun and it fits any space. Tiny ladder-back chairs, rockers, desks and trunks are charming accent pieces, as are conventional highchairs, toys and cradles. (Many cradles were made with solid sides and hoods to protect the child from drafts, since many people believed that night air promoted lung disorders.) Almost all these pieces were made of pine so that they would be lightweight, and easily moved about.

The Room That Moved Indoors

Country is great decorating for every room in the house. This is best proven by country's adaptability to a room that the settlers never even dreamed of—the bathroom. Progress has brought an abundance of sterility and plastic to the modern bathroom. Acrylic and stainless steel have replaced generously proportioned cast-iron bathtubs with brass and porcelain faucets. But a bathroom does not have to look mechanical or antiseptic. With the right fixtures and accessories, your bathroom can look as warm and comfortable as the rest of your country home.

If you're lucky enough to own a house with an old tub and sink, don't remove them. There are plenty of restorers who can help you with the repairs that might be necessary. You're not likely to find such interesting shapes and materials in any contemporary plumbing fixtures. Plain hardwood floors with a protective finish, cork or quarry floor tiles make for a country feeling in the bath. Wooden towel racks, wicker baskets, jars and bottles on open shelves and an old framed mirror helps to create a warm ambience. Solid oak toilet seats with brass hinges, available from man-

ufacturers in Northwood, New Hampshire, provide much more natural comfort than chilly plastic or ludicrous foam-filled seats. If you have a pull-chain toilet, keep it. Pull-chain toilets use only two gallons of water as opposed to the eight gallons used by most modern flush toilets. So once again, old wins out over new even in the most modern of rooms.

In reaction to the emphasis on high-tech furniture and homes that look like factories, we are seeing a renewed appreciation for the unpretentious and uncomplicated styles of the past. People are collecting country furniture precisely because it is honestly constructed and simple in design. The furniture and artifacts of long ago are being reborn and promise to bring us more years of comfort and use. That's what the country style is all about.

5
Country Homes

We travelled across the nation, from the southern shore of Long Island to the rugged coast of Washington in search of unique country houses. Each of these folks—the Raycrafts, the Lawrences, the Sullivans, the Muessels, and the Weisses—have brought country into their homes.

RUSTIC RENOVATION

When Jeff Weiss and Yolande Flesch found this 1860 Victorian farm house, the place was a mess. The floors sagged, the window frames were rotten, and both the plumbing and wiring was faulty. They gutted the inside, stripped the linoleum from the hardwood floors and transformed a ramshackle beach cottage into a beautiful weekend retreat.

Don Somerset, the master craftsman and designer in charge of the renovation, wanted to keep the Victorian flavor of the house and so he retained the gingerbread supports in the front and matched them in the back. The boxy first floor was opened up and transformed into two separate spaces, the eat-in kitchen and the airy living room-dining room. The windows were replaced by Anderson double-glazed glass and framed in pine. They used original wall beams from the house to frame the doorways and ceiling beams were installed over a stucco ceiling.

In the kitchen, Jeff and Yolande have successfully combined old-fashioned character with modern efficiency to create a comfortable, functional kitchen. The ceiling joists were exposed and they installed custom-built cedar and ma-

hogany cabinets topped with quarry tile. A handsome maple Hoosier cabinet, c. 1930, stands on the wide-plank pine floor and complements the easy-to-clean stainless steel stove and dishwasher. Their collections of depression glass and kitchen antiques are displayed on pine shelves and the walls are decorated with prints by local artists. To keep things cool, they installed a ceiling fan with wooden blades. French doors lead to a brick patio where they like to take their meals.

All eyes are drawn to the brilliant star-shaped rag rug that covers the oak floor in the living room. The contemporary white couch fits in naturally with the rattan chairs, c. 1930, and the colorful Moroccan rugs. The old walnut table in the dining room is covered with an antique lace table cloth and an old maple chest was converted into a sideboard. The custom-made cedar door opens into the TV/guest room.

Stripped pine stairs lead to the upstairs bedrooms where Jeff and Yolande have used antiques to accent their informal decorating scheme. A painted pine chest, found on the streets of New York, and quilts purchased at the Brimfield Fair add graceful touches to the master bedroom. The turn-of-the-century stripped pine chest in the children's room works well with the triple pipe bunk beds. The bathroom complete with an old tub, bidet and water closet, is all cedar and pine. From their bedroom, Jeff and Yolande can see the duck pond which was donated to the town by Mrs. Russell Sage.

Jeff and Yolande scrubbed down a ramshackle farm house and transformed it into a comfortable country retreat. The renovation was completed in just nine months.

In the kitchen and dining room, old ceiling beams were used to frame the doorways, the pine cabinets were custom-made to match and the linoleum that covered the floor was removed and quickly discarded.

A turn-of-the-century stripped pine chest, rag rug and handmade quilts give the children's bedroom its old-fashioned character.

In the bathroom, an amply-proportioned tub stands on a wide-plank pine floor.

An unusual star-shape rag rug and handmade quilt enhance the contemporary country decor in the living room.

LIVING WITH ANTIQUES

Carol and Don Raycraft have been collecting for 15 years and their home is a treasure chest of original American antiques.

The old horse barn, which had been in the family for three generations, was built in 1858 and converted by the Raycrafts into a comfortable live-in museum for their possessions. The stone used for the structure was originally brought to the downstate Illinois area from Joliet by convicts helping to build the Chicago/St. Louis Railroad.

Except for the handsome Chippendale loveseat, there's nothing new in the Raycraft living room. The old sea captain's chest dates from about 1825, and the gathering baskets on either side of the loveseat are nearly as old. The simple Shaker chair, c. 1850–1870, has a rush seat and is one of the largest made by the sect. The old "step-back" cupboard still wears its original red paint, as does the cradle which dates from about 1830. Originally purchased for their third son, the cradle now rocks his grandmother's 70-year-old doll, dressed in a Shaker child's cloak. The old wooden floor is covered with a turn-of-the-century braided rug.

The Raycrafts know how to use detail: a blue-gray combination dry sink and bucket bench, c. 1850, is complemented by a turn-of-the-century checkerboard and hand-carved dough bowl filled with red-ware and wooden plates; a stack of Shaker boxes (all of which were purchased at one time) with their original paint stands between an early Shaker weaver's chair and a rare Shaker broom made of splint; and a "rocker/roller horse," c. 1875, with its original hair, stands at the entrance to a room with a tidy display of pantry boxes, firkins and Shaker berry boxes. A

rare Windsor cheese drainer makes an unusual wall hanging.

Recently converted from attic space, the eldest son's bedroom now has new wooden walls, ceiling and floor. The surprisingly comfortable New England rope bed stands on another turn-of-the-century braided rug. The immigrant's trunk at the foot of the bed was found in New York State. The early eagle tavern sign which crowns the bed still bears its original paint, as does the early toy cannon. The proud wooden letters declaring ownership are from a turn-of-the-century grocery.

Charming rocker/roller horse leads into a sitting room filled with antiques; the old bucket bench, now used as a wood box, still has its original paint.

The awesome Raycraft home stands magnificent on the Midwestern prairie.

How easily a collection of old items, simply arranged, can turn a portion of a wall into a visual memory of days gone by!

The reproduction Chippendale loveseat fits in perfectly with the antiques in the Raycraft living room.

A stack of Shaker boxes in this stone corner extends the warmth of wood and the color of the rug right up to the ceiling.

With the right accessories, this child's bedroom achieves a rugged bunkhouse quality without sacrificing cleanliness or comfort.

SELF-MADE COUNTRY

In 1972, Jim Lawrence tired of the city, moved to an island off the coast of Washington and lived in a tepee while he built his neo-Gothic country home. He now shares his compact 14′ x 20′ house with his adopted son Aku and Aku's pet rabbit, Rasta.

Jim is a self-taught carpenter, scuba diver and farmer—Tanzy, the healthy-looking Holstein grazing on the front lawn, provides milk for the calves he sells to market. The ingeniously designed house was planned with function in mind. Jim says, with quiet humility, "My house works." Like the early American settlers, Jim used the materials at hand—all the lumber used is native to the island—to build a comfortable, ecologically sound living space. The entire structure was constructed for $800.

Jim paneled his living room and bedroom with an old red cedar fence he purchased for $45. The shelves are also made of red cedar, the handsome floor of hemlock. Jim built the beechwood steps that lead to the bedroom in one night. His industry was a product of fatigue: "I was tired of climbing a ladder," he says dryly. The air-tight Fisher stove heats the

entire house.

From his bedroom, Jim has a lofty view of his property. The hand-embroidered sconce that provides the reading light was made by his mother. Jim stitched the quilt himself.

In a country home, a simple metal cup can conjure up all kinds of magic tricks.

Jim describes his kitchen as "uneventful but functional." The counter is made from old maple floorboards and the sink is actually half a barrel sunk and secured into the counter. The kitchen is filled with stoneware, spatterware and other things Jim collects.

The sod roof on the chicken coop was an experiment and turned out to be a successful alternative to more common and expensive roofing. Inspired by the Norwegian vernacular tradition, the roof is discreetly incorporated into the environment and blossoms in the springtime.

A solitary cow grazes before this gregarious wooden house nestled in the forest of the northwest.

This side building uses an old sodhouse technique for natural insulation.

With its airy windows, this lofty bedroom lets dreamers imagine they are sleeping beneath the stars.

44

This modern homesteader's cozy, cluttered living room combines rustic, natural elements and rough-hewn wooden stairs.

Strong soap, strong hands, and a strong pine sink will get any pot clean.

COUNTRY SOLAR

Bob Muessel trekked through the mountains of Colorado for three years before he found the site for his magnificent country home. The house he shares with his wife Marilyn is cut into the side of a hill and stands on a foundation of river rock. The solar panels and windows face south-southwest so that in the winter, the sunshine reaches all the way to the back of the house and in the summer, direct sunlight falls only on the greenhouse. Sunshine is "captured" by the rocks and the flagstone and tile floors and can supply heat for two to three days. Supplementary heat is provided by a wood-burning stove and baseboard electric. To insure maximal heat circulation, Bob designed the house without walls.

Bob wanted a rough, natural look (" 'crude and rude' that's my name") so he chose unfinished native spruce for his house which he describes as a southwest Indian/ Mexican post and beam structure. He chose a tropical motif for the front door to reflect the sunny interior. Martha Kendall fashioned the glass and the hardware on the door and throughout the house was tooled by Ted Titcomb.

The greenhouse is an integral part of the house. Easy to maintain, insect resistant succulents which can withstand hours of direct sunlight fill the stucco planters. The deep red design (the color was selected for its absorptive quality) imitates the mountains beyond.

The old oak dining room set, which includes leather-covered chairs dates from the turn of the century. The alcove is decorated with hand-painted Mexican plates, pewter candlesticks and Mexican pottery. The gracious cabinet was designed by Bob's brother and finished with knobs from Mexico.

A circular stairway leads to the master bedroom. Two double closets (not seen) are on the north wall—the clothes stored within further insulate the house. The iron bed frame, c. 1910, was imported from Michigan, as was the old traveller's trunk, which was once owned by Marilyn's great grandfather. The beautiful, claw foot bathtub was repainted on the outside, but it still has the original enamel finish on the inside. And guess what? Like everything else in this splendidly designed country house, it works.

The stained glass design in a rustic door adds a touch of tropical sun and color.

This efficently angled and open-faced house was designed and built by the owner.

46

As in old-fashioned, single-room cabins, this room combines bed and bath before a panoramic view of the Colorado Rockies.

Cactus and adobe motifs bring the southwest desert indoors for a relaxed, patio effect.

This alcove, styled and arranged with informal simplicity, creates chapel-like serenity.

THE PERFECT MIX OF OLD AND NEW

In 1977, Lucy and Bill Sullivan bought an isolated piece of property with a pond. It was Lucy's dream. She had always wanted a place to build a comfortable, country-style home. The house she and her husband share was completely designed and decorated by Lucy and the entire project took a scant five months. If she had it to do all over again, Lucy says she wouldn't make a single change.

Like the old, common-room kitchens of the past, the Sullivan kitchen is large enough for food preparation and dining. The brick fireplace which now accommodates a stove and counter space is adorned with antique kitchen implements: polished copper molds, sauce pans and kettles, sturdy iron ladles and pastry cutters and pretty tin cookie cutters. The wooden rack on the back wall was originally a meat rack. An old kerosene lamp, wooden fruit bowl and biscuit cutters stand on an old Irish pine work table. The floor is quarry tile cut in the shape of bricks. In the eating area, the Sullivans use good-quality reproductions to give their table an old-fashioned, rustic look. The table is set with new, old-looking pewter

flatware, goblets and plate liners, and a new quilt is used as a table cloth. The chairs, china and lamp are new as well and add to the nostalgic look. The Early American cupboard and pine shelf hold an assortment of antique kitchenware and ceramic and metal cooking molds. The old metal bird cage which Lucy uses as a planter adds a lighthearted, whimsical touch.

The Sullivans have decorated their guest room with their favorite antique shop finds. The old walnut night table, c. 1850, matches the walnut bed frame, c. 1860. An antique quilt, on which sits an amusing pair of old stuffed toys, covers the bed. The spinning wheel and chair are probably from the 19th century, as is the basket which contains dried wildflowers.

The rustic-looking door latches and hinges are reproductions.

The upstairs bathroom is an attractive mix of old and new. The recently purchased dark wood chest is topped by a marble look-alike Corian® sink and counter and is illuminated by reproduction wall lamps. The old rocker has been in the family for generations, but the handsome braided rug was purchased last year. The antique wooden walker, now innovatively used as a towel rack, stands on stained pine board flooring.

Warm light enhances this home's proud stature on the edge of a pond.

50

An old-fashioned quilt, a cushioned rocker, and an antique spinning wheel turn this attic nook into a child's room that evokes the mood of yesteryear.

The quiet warmth of wood tones is easily enhanced by the judicious use of rich browns in curtains and wallpaper.

A suggestion of the cozy bedrooms upstairs creeps down the stairway with this handcrafted quilt.

As in farm kitchens of old, this 20th century "fireplace" uses its cheeks: an oven goes in the left, a refrigerator in the right.

This rustic bathroom has the feel of an old western hotel.

Fabulous Country Kitchens

The kitchen is the perfect room in which to put together a warm, old-fashioned country look, reminiscent of the Early American farm kitchen. This room has always been the traditional center of a farm family's house, a place for cooking and sharing a meal with the farm hands, for the Saturday night bath and for family prayers. It was constantly alive with activity. Women churned their own butter, packed it into tubs and shaped it or decorated it with pretty geometric, floral and animal designs. Fruits and vegetables were "put up" in the fall and bread was baked, perhaps a dozen loaves at a time, once a week. Every farmwife made her own scrumptious desserts—fruit pies were the national favorite. When a neighbor appeared, he was usually offered a piece of pie and invited to set a spell.

Like the rural kitchens of the past, today's country kitchens should be comfortable places where friends and family can congregate for casual meals and informal conversation, where children can play and where cats and dogs can nap. Even if you lack the space for such a kitchen, you can at least achieve its spirit of friendly informality.

This spacious, early-Pennsylvania kitchen, peeking into a plain but elegant dining room, has been rewired for electric candles and a refrigerator.

The old-time crafts of candle making, basket weaving, butter churning and good home cooking suggest the warmth of human activity that fills this cozy kitchen.

The Hub Of The House

In most modern homes, food preparation, eating space, laundry, utilities and storage are partitioned into separate areas, but in older homes, where the kitchen was truly the hub of the house, these were all incorporated into one large undivided room. The kitchen was cluttered with wooden tubs, kegs, barrels and cases containing food and household supplies. Baskets of woven straw and earthenware jugs and storage pots filled the shelves. Glass bottles and jars stood on windowsills and tin and copper molds and pans hung from the ceiling beams or hooks in the walls. The kitchen constantly resounded with the inviting cacophony of chopping, beating, whipping, stirring and the clank of heavy utensils.

In the earliest American kitchens, the fireplace was the dominant feature of the room. It was made of stone or brick and was often large enough to roast a whole animal. The chimney was made of wood and daubed on the inside with clay. A wooden lug pole, and later a wrought-iron chimney crane, or reckon, hung from the inside of the chimney and cooking pots were suspended by hooks over the fire. A housewife could cook a whole meal in one pot by placing various foods in a jar or linen bag and placing the bag into a cauldron filled with boiling water. The crane could be swung in and out from the fire, making it easier to remove the kettle. Ovens were built into the cheeks of the fireplace and used for baking. One of the most common kitchen utensils was the Dutch oven, a baking kettle with a tight-fitting lid which was placed directly into the fire and covered with coals for slow cooking. The hearth was cluttered with pot hooks, skewers, trivets, peels and long-handled forks. If the housewife was lucky, she owned an ingenious contraption called the roasting kitchen, a metal box on legs which had an internal spit. The side near the fire was totally open and the door facing the cook could be raised to check and baste the meat.

A Real Workroom

The Early American kitchen was a real workroom filled with tables, stools, utensils, wash benches (there were no sinks), powdering tubs for salting meats, meal chests, cheese presses, a spinning wheel, perhaps a loom and probably a pallet bed for the oldest man in the house. Work tables and food preparation surfaces were scattered about the room. The largest table usually stood in the center of the room. Most of the food was prepared here and it was here that the family sat down to eat.

Naturally, the 17th-, 18th- and 19th-century homemaker had many more tools and implements than we do today since virtually everything was done at home. Her workload was strenuous—she ground her own spices, prepared setting agents from animal bones, made rinsing agents from ale and polishes and washing compounds from beeswax and ashes—and tools were created to ease her labor. She used a milk strainer to retrieve flies, twigs, straw and dirt that fell into the pail at milking time; a sugar cutter to nip off a bit of the sweet cone; a twirler, a long, wooden rod with a star-shaped head to mix ingredients; and many

56

other instruments like toddy sticks, apple peelers, salamanders, olive stoners, hullers, nutmeg grinders and lemon squeezers that a 20th-century homemaker does not need. Because food was not premeasured like the food we buy today, a housewife kept scales, weights and measures within easy reach.

The average diet of the early American was much heavier and certainly more limited than ours. Corn meal, boiled meats, vegetables and stew were basics. Hasty pudding, a sodden composition of corn meal mush and milk with boiled meat or fish, was a common dish. When vegetables were available, the mush was surrounded by boiled corn or carrots. Main dishes were served in large wooden plates called trenchers. Most trenchers were made of a single piece of wood. Par-

ents usually shared one trencher and children another. Forks were not a part of Early American life: the little finger and thumb were used as pinchers and the remaining three as a scoop. The first settlers did use marrow spoons to scoop the marrow from bones (an Early American delicacy). Pie was the standard dessert (in the winter, dozens of pies were baked at one time and stored in the snow) and grog or cider was served in wooden cups called noggins. Soups were also popular and plentiful and sauces were used to extend the basic food dish. (Sauces were also good for "sopping up" with a chunk of hearty bread.) Almost every family grew their own produce, which was harvested in the fall. What was not immediately consumed was put up for later use.

Fortunately, today's homemaker does not have to rely on milk strainers and olive stoners, but all of us are discovering the decorative value of these old gadgets and tableware and are ornamenting our kitchens with displays of rustic woodenware, solid stoneware and sturdy cast-iron.

These heavy iron utensils can reach deep into a pot or fireplace to poke a rib roast or ladle a sip of thick, hot soup.

The Old-Fashioned Cookstove

Before modernism turned the kitchen into a laboratory, the kitchen was truly the hub of the house, and the stove or fireplace was the place where people gathered to stay warm and feel the fire's glow.

Although iron cookstoves were available at the end of the 18th century, they were not standard kitchen equipment until the middle of the 19th century. The stove was essential to the life of the family; it was the last thing to be taken down at moving time and the first thing to be set up. It was used for heating, cooking, boiling water, baking, drying clothes and for warming a newborn lamb or a shivering child.

Unlike today's stoves, the cookstoves of the 19th century did not have regulating thermometers. Cooking was done "by guess and by golly"—country cooks knew how to improvise and experi-

ment. A farm wife in 1845 suggested the following method for regulating oven temperature: "for pies, cakes, and white bread . . . hold your arm in while you count 40; for brown bread, meats, beans, Indian puddings, and pumpkin pies, it should be hotter, so that you can only hold it in while you count 20." It's not surprising that kitchen clocks were first advertised to "promote punctuality" for "that good understanding which sometimes subsists between the clock and the cook."

———————————— ▸•◂ ————————————

The Modern Cookstove

Many country homeowners today are discovering the pleasure of cooking on a modern wood-burning stove. The wood-burning stove is one of the most ecologically sound tools ever invented: it can, with wood you've gathered yourself, cook your food and heat your house and water all at the same time. If you are thinking about installing a new oven, consider instead a wood-burning stove. Besides being energy efficient, it is self-cleaning and a great slow cooker.

A wood-burning stove is composed of a firebox, an oven, a cooking surface and some stove pipe.

When Spring arrives, the windows go up and the wood-burning stove rests for awhile.

Some more elaborate models have a warming oven, but none have broilers. The rondels on the cooking surface are similar to the burners on a gas stove, but the heat is not controlled by a knob which raises and lowers the flame. Unlike a gas stove, the entire surface of a wood-burning stove can be used for cooking.

Because the cook must continually tend the fire, it's a good idea to keep utensils such as metal hooks (to remove the rondels), pokers and pot holders within easy reach. With a little practice, it's easy to make a good cooking fire. All you have to do is crumple a few pieces of newspaper and some kindling and throw them into the firebox. Make sure the damper is open. Start the fire and fill, but don't stuff, the firebox with wood (the spaces between and around the wood keep the fire going). When the wood is burning well, gently add a few pieces of heavier wood. If you need to make a quick, hot fire, add a piece of softwood, like pine. When the fire is going strong, close the flue slightly and add a split log. The stove is now hot and will maintain heat as long as you add a medium-sized piece of wood from time to time.

Cast-iron pots work especially well with a wood-burning stove and fit in perfectly with country decor. These sturdy utensils hold and spread heat, and their heavy, tight-fitting lids help retain heat. Wood-burning stoves are especially good for slow-cooking and steaming. If you bake in your stove, remember that the top of whatever you are baking darkens first in a wood-burning stove,

From behind these two porcelain oven doors seaps the rich aroma of homemade pies and cakes.

rather than the bottom, as in gas ovens. Foods must be turned and placed in different areas of the oven in order to bake evenly. Use your intuition and you should become an expert in no time.

A Woman's Work Was Never Done

It's easy to romanticize the rural life of our ancestors. But "life was no picnic," as one man who grew up on a farm in the Middle West during the early years of the 20th century recalled. Especially for the woman of the house. Simple, easy and convenient were not words applied to the kitchen. Another laconic old-timer remembered, "You didn't just push a button."

"My memory holds no picture of my mother sitting with folded hands," wrote a slightly more loquacious former farm boy. The farmhouse kitchen was cold in the winter until after the morning fire was lighted, and hot in the summer until the stove cooled off. The woman of the house engaged in chores unknown to, and perhaps unimagined by, the 20th-century homemaker. She smoked, dried, pickled, preserved, canned, bottled, cured, churned, brewed, weaved, washed, ironed and sewed. She made fuel, food, candles, soap, clothes and medicines. There was no indoor plumbing (water was carried from a river or well or pumped from a cistern), no refrigeration (most American farmhouses were not electrified until after World War II) and no central heat. And nobody had Brillo in the old days; pots and pans were scraped clean with a putty knife and fingernails.

But like their male counterparts, these anonymous women kept a stiff upper lip and managed their rugged existences with a certain amount of pluck and cheerfulness. These instructions, by an unnamed woman, offer some idea of what our rural ancestors were like:

Receet for Washing Clothes
Anonymous

1. bild fire in backyard to het kettle of rain water.

2. set tubs so smoke won't blow in eyes if wind is pert.

3. shave one hol cake lie sope in bilin water.

4. sort things, make 3 piles
   1 pile white, 1 pile cullord,
   1 pile werk britches and rags.

5. stir flour in cold water to smooth, then thin down with bilin water.

6. rub dirty spots on board, scrub hard. then bile. rub cullord but don't bile—just rench and starch.

7. take white things out of kettle with broomstick handel. then rench, blew and starch.

8. spread tee towels on grass.

9. hang old rags on fence.

10. pore rench water in flower bed.

11. scrub porch with hot sopy water.

12. turn tubs upside down.

13. go put on cleen dress—smooth hair with side combs. brew cup of tea and rest and rock a spell and count blessings.

A Social History of The Kitchen

More than any other room in the house, the kitchen mirrors the great social changes of the last 300 years. The first kitchens were called "keeping rooms," a term of medieval origin. It was often the only room and, because it was certainly the only room that was heated, the family spent most of their waking hours there. The fireplace, which was often eight to ten feet wide, was the focal point of the room. The most common methods of cooking were boiling and roasting, and it was not unusual to see a cook with singed eyebrows and a perspiring forehead.

THE INVENTIVE 19TH CENTURY

Kitchens expanded with the frontier. In the 19th century, as Americans prospered, the middle class hired people to help in the kitchen. In order to isolate nasty cooking odors and unpleasant sounds, the kitchen was placed downstairs, outside, or anywhere away from the dining area. In New England, the kitchen was usually placed in an ell in the back of the house. In the South, the kitchen was usually in a separate outbuilding.

The Industrial Revolution changed the cooking and eating habits of Americans. Sea and rail routes improved, providing urbanites with fresh produce almost year 'round. New methods of feeding livestock were developed and for the first

Cast iron utensils, an old-fashioned paper dispenser and a heavy metal room heater, all collected from the past, accent this unpretentious kitchen.

time, fresh meat was available all year long. New synthetic materials were invented which helped lighten the housewife's load, but ironically, spring cleaning was not recorded until the 19th century, when the soot from gas and oil lamps created the need for this annual ritual.

THE HIGH-TECH 20TH CENTURY

At the turn of this century, linoleum was patented and cast-iron pots were enameled. The gas stove replaced the coal- or wood-burning stove and food was taken from the shelf and put in a separate space called the larder or pantry. A family might own one china cabinet, but otherwise the kitchen was still cluttered with various shelves and tables for preparation and storage.

World War I precipitated a dramatic upheaval in the way Americans lived. The servants of the 19th century found better wages in the new factories and the middle class found replacements in new gadgets. Electric ranges, which had been invented in 1890, gained popularity in the 1920s and refrigerators were installed in most homes by the end of the 1930s. Large containers such as salt-glazed stoneware crocks, formerly used for food storage, were no longer necessary. The refrigerator had taken their place. Because the servantless middle class housewife did not want to travel the long distance from the 19th-century cooking area to the dining room, the kitchen was returned to a place closer to the eating area.

In 1900, the Hoosier Cabinet, designed to bring factory-like efficiency to the kitchen, was patented. Housewives embraced it. This compact unit was designed to store all the equipment necessary to prepare a meal. The cabinet included compartments above and below; a flour bin and sifter; a tilt jar for sugar; jars for spices, coffee and tea; a pull-out shelf for extra working space; sectioned drawers; and a metal drawer to store bread.

Technological advances further compacted kitchens after World War II. Mass-produced, built-in cabinets and easy-to-clean, laminated plastic countertops were developed. Architects revered Le Corbusier, who decreed that a house was "a machine to live in," and every new house was designed with clinical precision. With built-in storage space, big kitchens were unnecessary. And with the new frozen convenience foods, meals could be prepared quickly and almost surreptitiously.

TODAY'S COUNTRY KITCHEN

But in the wake of the sterile technology of the 1950s "dream kitchen," we are seeing a renewed interest in the warm, friendly country kitchen of our ancestors. Architects now recall the rest of Le Corbusier's words: "Since men also have hearts, we have also tried to insure that men with hearts would be able to live happily in our houses," and are designing kitchens which combine efficiency with the charm of yesterday. Fatigued by gadgetry and sleek, impersonal design, we are looking to country to provide us with warmth and efficiency.

Today, we are returning to an almost medieval conception of the kitchen as the central family room. We cook, eat and entertain in the kitchen. Children play in the kitchen and adults gather there for conversation. As in the rural kitchens of earlier times, each member of the family takes part in the kitchen chores.

After years of TV dinners and foods spiked with preservatives, country cooks are rediscovering their taste buds. Good fresh food, prepared and served in the traditional way, as well as quality

kitchen equipment, have regained an important place in our lives. Once again, kitchen shelves are lined with home-canned peaches and tomatoes.

Making Your Country Kitchen Work

The idea behind a country kitchen is to combine the convenience and efficiency of modern equipment with the warmth and hospitality of the past. There's no reason not to have a Cuisinart, dishwasher or garbage disposal. Such aids are work-savers and serve a good purpose.

The layout of the kitchen should provide enough room to facilitate the job of food preparation and still accommodate a family gathering. The key words are function and simplicity: things should work well and look attractive.

According to a study conducted at Cornell University, the efficiency of a kitchen is determined by the location of its work areas. The most efficient arrangement is: refrigerator, work surface, stove, work surface, sink, work surface. This basic sequence can be adapted to any kitchen layout; a single line, L-shape, U-shape or galley configuration. The size and dimension of the room will usually determine which layout is chosen.

If you are designing or remodeling your kitchen, these simple guidelines should help. Plan on 1 1/2' of counter space by the refrigerator to facilitate loading and unloading. Allow 2' of counter space beside the range (a wooden insert or ceramic tiles will protect the surface from hot dishes). Most designers recommend about 4' of countertop space for the preparation of foods and about 3' of space on either side of the sink for dirty dishes and preparation.

If you are about to remodel an older house that dates from the era when kitchens weren't that spacious, there are ways to enlarge it. Consider knocking out a wall to incorporate a back hallway as part of the kitchen space. The traffic through the back of the house is likely to be through the kitchen anyway. Or give away that old upright gas stove and substitute a counter model, using the space for a seating area. If there isn't room for a free-standing table, have one built in with hinges that hook up against the wall and let down when you need it. Overhead, install an interesting and decorative light fixture that pulls down close to the table and gives the intimate effect of an old-fashioned table lamp. As a last resort, you can always move the refrigerator to a back hallway to make more space in the kitchen. It's not a perfect solution, but it has been done.

An Old-Fashioned Pantry

In an old house, many people use the pantry or larder to enlarge the kitchen. But don't waste the larder. Because it is close to, but away from the heat of the kitchen, it is the perfect place to keep fresh-killed chickens, hams and other meats which do not do well in the refrigerator (where extreme temperature does not allow for maturation). It's also a good storage space for vegetables, fruits,

An old washtub set on top of a wooden icebox makes a handy and attractive container for a collection of wooden kitchen utensils.

sausage and cheeses. Cut flowers will stay fresher longer if stored there overnight. Use any extra space for bulky packages of dry goods, vases and seldom-used pots and pans.

Adding Country Flair

Even in a city apartment, it's surprisingly easy and inexpensive to create the look of a country kitchen. Country flair can be added with the simplest of touches: a painted dado, a door of pine planking with wrought-iron strap hinges, pine baseboards or a beamed ceiling. It doesn't take much, and most of what you need can be found at flea markets, junkyards or in your own attic.

Country is the easiest of looks to put together because you don't really have to work for the effect. All you need are some open shelves to show off your pretty china and your homemade preserves or a basket to fill with dried flowers and use as a centerpiece to achieve the country look.

COUNTRY ACCENTS

It's all a matter of detail. Any kitchen can be warmed by a display of shining copperware (a coating of polyurethane will prevent tarnish) or polished brassware. Almost anything that was once useful can be adapted as a decorative accent in today's country kitchens. Pieces of spatterware, for example, now too fragile for everyday use, look pretty on a windowsill. Gizzard baskets, once used to transport vegetables from the fields, can be hung from hooks in the ceiling beams. Tin candlesticks with slim tapers make attractive decorative accents, and old wooden bowls can be used to hold fruit or dried flowers. Toddy dogs, apple

peelers and olive stoners make pretty arrangements in an old pine hutch or on a plain open shelf. Pot racks, trivets, cast-iron toasters and skewers, once necessary for fireplace cookery, can be displayed in a modern kitchen and provide just the rustic touch you want. Many of these can be found at flea markets and junkyards, but if you can't find the piece you're looking for, it's sure to be available from one of the many reliable craftspeople working today.

A cheerful array of indoor color and outdoor greenery provide a bright, airy setting for kitchen tasks.

A country kitchen is a cheerful clutter of odds and ends. Anything from crockery jars, candle molds, wooden noggins, salt boxes, milk strainers, muffin tins, braided rugs and wooden casks can give you the look.

Use your imagination to fill your kitchen with objects that are both functional and attractive. Recycle old materials: turn an old chicken feeder into a unique hanging lamp, fit an antique armoire with modern, laminated shelves, use old Bible racks as compact holders for cookbooks. Hutch-buffets, cupboards and wheeled servers can all serve as attractive and utilitarian space savers. A dry sink makes a stylish container for green plants. These cabinets, usually made with an open tray top, lined with zinc (some rural historians swear by the apocryphal notion that our modern word sink comes from the slurring of zinc), were used for kitchen chores before the era of indoor plumbing. Most were made of pine or poplar, but occasionally craftsmen made them in oak, chestnut, walnut or cherry.

This refurbished pine cabinet and chest of drawers give this kitchen its old-fashioned country feeling.

Pine and brick create a warm background for the happy profusion of goods and utensils that give this small kitchen character.

Dry goods in their packages of different shapes and sizes, often with colorful labels, can look attractive set out on open shelves. Eggs cook better and their shells won't crack if kept at room temperature—so put them in a wire basket or a crockery bowl and make a pretty country still-life. For the storage of other ingredients, such as flour and sugar, consider old stoneware crocks or wooden boxes. Find an old salt box and hang it within easy reach of the stove for last-minute seasoning.

CABINETS AND COUNTERTOPS

Cabinets are usually the largest investment when creating or restructuring a kitchen, but in a country kitchen, the mood is one of openness rather than concealment. Open shelves are both functional and attractive; however, many people object to clutter. If you are one of these, and are installing new cabinets, keep in mind that wood grains and finishes evoke a natural, country mood.

Countertops can be made country by using butcher block or ceramic tiles. Even Formica, if accented by natural materials such as baskets or earthenware, will lend itself to the old-fashioned rustic spirit.

Country means natural finishes, and that applies to floors as well as countertops and cabinets. If you have a solid wood floor, sand it down to its

Trimmed and lined with richly colored tiles, the storage areas of this serviceable kitchen conceal their contents while leaving them in plain view.

original finish and cover it with a matte type of polyurethane to protect its natural character. If you wish, you can stencil the floors, like the early Americans did, before you apply the polyurethane. If you are installing a new floor, consider quarry or ceramic tiles, bricks, slate or stone—all provide a country look.

Old-time country kitchens were big kitchens. To make yours seem larger, paint the ceiling a light color. Use gloss or semi-gloss in a light color like white, ivory, apricot-beige or lemon-yellow. If you're using wallpaper, avoid a busy pattern. A plain paper makes a room look larger and will make a better background for whatever you are going to hang there.

A country kitchen means natural lighting. If your existing kitchen is short on windows, consider installing a skylight. Although skylights are certainly not authentic to old-time country kitchens, they do keep to a minimum the harsh, artificial lighting favored by modern designers.

Caring For Your Kitchen Treasures

Now that you've filled your kitchen with old-fashioned treasures and near-treasures, you'll need to know how to take care of them. Old pottery, for example, may not be ovenproof, and you should avoid subjecting it to sudden temperature changes. If the glaze is cracked, the pottery will pick up food stains. Stoneware is ovenproof and will not stain if the glaze is cracked. Aluminum is light and easy to clean and will not rust or tarnish. But it does pit easily. Aluminum is best cleaned by boiling tomatoes, rhubarb or other acidic fruits in the container. If you find an old cast-iron trivet that you'd like to use in the kitchen, remove the rust with steel wool. Unfinished cast iron should be seasoned with salad oil. Clean cast iron with detergent, dry it thoroughly and oil it again before storing. Enamelware should be washed with nylon scourers and soaked in a weak bleach solution to remove stains. Avoid sudden temperature changes and knocks, as enameled pieces chip easily. Copper and brass can be polished with a commercial metal cleaner, or you can do it the old-fashioned way, by rubbing the piece every day with room-temperature buttermilk, whey or sour milk. Remove tarnish by rubbing the piece with half a lemon dipped in salt and vinegar. Treat old tinware gently—excessive cleaning will remove the tinplate and expose the iron. If food is really baked on, don't scour the piece, but soak it in soapy water. Let it air dry. Most old crockery will be damaged by the high temperature of dishwashers and should therefore be washed in warm water in a plastic bowl. Don't use abrasive cleaners—tea stains can be removed with a damp, salted cloth that has been dipped in bicarbonate of soda. When using old glassware, avoid sudden temperature changes. When pouring a hot liquid into an old cup, put a spoon in it first to prevent breakage. Because the rim is the weakest part of the glass, stemware should not be stored upside down. Narrow-necked containers can be cleaned by swilling them in a solution of vinegar water and salt. If you use your old woodenware, let it air dry after washing it in warm soapy water. Lemon juice will lighten cutting boards and stains can be removed with bleach (be sure to rinse the board after applying bleach). Woodenware used only for display should be protected with a coating of beeswax.

The future lies in country kitchens. Our renewed interest in country living is just one demonstration of our desire to return to the values of the past. As conservationists, we are learning to respect our environment and make constructive use of our natural resources. The generation brought up in country kitchens will once again discover the flavor of fresh food.

A Matter of Detail: Crafts and Collectibles

CRAFTS

Two hundred years ago, the crafts-man was an integral part of the social fabric, producing such daily necessities as pottery, glassware and furniture. The master crafts-man ran his own shop. He selected designs, many of them artful recreations of popular European models, determined prices and hired journeymen and apprentices to whom he imparted his skill, thus insuring the craft's continuance for another generation. Today, over a century after the industrial revolution made the artisan obsolete, we are witnessing a rebirth of crafts. A new generation is finding sustenance and beauty in handmade objects. Craft shops are becoming an increasingly common sight on back country roads and regional craft fairs are introducing thousands to the variety of goods currently being made.

There are many reasons for the resurgence of crafts. Certainly the "back to the land" movement, urging a way of life that recaptures the simplicity of the past, has drawn many people to these ex-

pressions of an earlier life. On a more complex level, crafts are a rebellion against the obsolescence and uniformity that characterize many of our factory-built goods. In fact, many of today's craftspeople are refugees from the industrial world. It is not uncommon to find potters who were once engineers, or glassblowers who until a few weeks ago were driving buses.

Like collectibles, crafts can enrich your decorative options. Some crafts are functional. Others are purely aesthetic, a testimony to the number of artists who have chosen to express themselves with crafts rather than in the traditional field of fine arts. You can fill your kitchen cupboard with hand-blown glass goblets and stoneware plates. In the morning you can sip coffee from earthenware mugs glazed to resemble snowflakes on a pane of glass.

POTTERY

Pottery is perhaps the most familiar of all the crafts. Handmade pottery is widely available and inexpensive, as it has been since colonial times, when the potter was one of the busiest artisans. Because pots sold for pennies, his livelihood depended on quick, error-free production. During the fall he dug for clay, searching by lakes and stream beds. Once it had been found, he would haul the clay back to his shop, break it into workable portions, wash it thoroughly and

roll it into large balls for storage and seasoning. Primitive kilns made firing a pot a time-consuming and potentially disastrous procedure. To make earthenware, the potter would feed his kiln fire for 36 hours until the temperature reached 1800 degrees fahrenheit. Then he would wait another 36 hours for the kiln to cool. Opening it too early would crack the pots.

Aside from technologically improved kilns, the basic pottery techniques are those of the first potters who arrived in Massachusetts in 1635. Then, as now, all pottery is produced by using one of four basic techniques:

1. The piece may be entirely built by coils or ropes of clay, one laid upon another and all pressed together before firing.

2. The pot can be thrown by placing the clay on a revolving potter's wheel—the method we traditionally associate with pottery.

3. The potter can model the clay by hand.

4. The potter can use a mold into which the wet clay is pressed. Some tableware is made using this process.

Once fashioned, the piece of pottery is placed within the kiln and baked. For some items like flowerpots, this completes the work. With others, a glaze is required. Glazes are usually applied with a brush or a sponge and then baked to a glasslike finish, making the porous clay durable and waterproof. There are three types of glazes: shiny,

semi-shiny and dull or matte. Today's potter commands a wide repertoire of glazes that can imbue bowls, jars, vases, mugs, cups, plates, figurines and sculpture with remarkable hues.

One distinctive type of pottery that has become very popular and expensive is the black pottery of the Hopi Indians. This black ware is linked with the name Maria Martinez, a Hopi potter who came to prominence in the 1930s. It features a polished black design on a black background. This effect is obtained by burnishing the entire piece with a smooth stone, then painting either the background or design with an unpolished coat of slip (liquid clay). The black color is created by the clay's reaction when oxygen is smothered from the area around the pot during the final stages of firing.

GLASSWARE

Rarer than pottery is contemporary glassware. Even during colonial times, glass was expensive and most glassblowers depended upon rich patrons for their sustenance. After glass-pressing machines were developed in the 1820s, hand-blown glass became the luxury item of a few manufacturers like Tiffany and Durant. Today, thanks to highly efficient furnaces and refractories, the glassblower is able to operate out of his own house.

Glass, with its smooth, translucent quality, has always fascinated.

Undoubtedly we owe its existence to one of those fortuitous accidents—the mixing of sand and ash at a high temperature—that have provided us with so many everyday objects. The earliest glass was made by the Egyptians. They wrapped hot threads around sand cores to create decorative beads. By the time of Christ, the Syrians were fashioning blown glass with a pipe, the same basic technique used by today's glassblowers to fashion the goblets, vases and paperweights found in craft stores and fairs. Special consideration should also be given to the glass sculptures favored by many glassblowers.

STAINED GLASS

If hand-blown glass has traveled the road from functional object to art, stained glass has done the reverse. The beauty of light pouring through colored glass seems to give a universal delight and the pictorial possibilities of stained glass have charmed many craftspeople. It was the Romans, using imported Egyptian expertise, who made the first stained glass. But

Panels of stained glass infuse this kitchen with a kaleidoscope of warm color.

77

the art reached its zenith in the medieval Christian cathedrals, where it was used to narrate biblical parables and provide striking tableaus at different times of the day. It wasn't until the Victorian era that stained glass began to appear outside the church, in private homes and public buildings.

STENCILING

The earliest American houses were simple structures built around the fireplace. As accommodations became roomier and the colonists began to have the leisure to contemplate creature comforts, a number of strategies were devised to decorate the blank walls of their houses. The cheapest and most convenient method was a coat of paint. Those with money hired itinerant painters who stenciled designs on the walls, floors and ceilings. The stencils were usually patterns cut from parchment or linen. A favorite colonial motif was a fruit basket filled with apples, pears, grapes and leaves. After the Revolution, the American eagle became popular, a symbol of the nation's pride and ambition. By the

Hand-painted pine chests are considered real finds by country collectors.

1830s, the common thistle was extensively used.

A variation of stenciling called for a design to be drawn on a plaster wall and coated with glue. Then, chopped dyed wool was pressed into the glue to form colorful patterns that resembled cut velvet. Another decorative technique was to paint murals on plastered walls in emulation of French wallpaper. The drawing room, the dining room or the hall might be chosen to receive such murals, which were usually landscapes. Itinerant painters, armed with stencils and sketchbooks filled with mural designs, traveled the colonies. Many of their landscapes can be found in the mansions of the Hudson River Valley.

Stencils were also used to brighten up chairs, beds, chests, mirrors and cupboards. Tin objects such as trays, boxes and pitchers also received the treatment.

There are still stencilers plying their trade, some boasting the artistic expertise to cover your ceiling with unusual designs, others offering an array of traditional colonial motifs. You can also purchase do-it-yourself stencil kits, but be careful. Choose something bright and imaginative.

WALL HANGINGS

Today, quilts, tapestries, Indian blankets and fiber wall hangings are widely used to accent a blank wall. Tapestry weaving has been common since the middle ages,

when the famous Unicorn tapestries were first produced. In Spain, tapestries were woven from cartoons by Rubens and Goya. Nowadays, you can find tapestries by Picasso and Miro, as well as reproductions of classical themes. More familiar than tapestries are the woven blankets of the Western Indians. Many people consider these the most beautiful blankets in the world and even 100 years ago, cowboys were going into debt to purchase one.

Although the Zuni and the Hopi have made some appealing blankets, most enthusiasts seek out Navajo textiles. The Navajo

weavers work on an upright loom of their own invention and employ natural dies and wool from their own sheep. Before the turn of the century, they made blankets both for their own use and as trade goods. These were usually rectangular and vertically striped, although certain more elaborate pieces, called chief's blankets, were squarish in shape.

Since 1900, the Navajo have made a wide variety of rugs, some pictorial, some geometric, but all highly collectible. Indian rugs and blankets are today considered art forms to be hung alongside the finest modern paintings.

RUGS

Just as the earliest walls were blank, so the early floors were sand. This had advantages: they could be changed whenever they got dirty. Only the very wealthy could afford the Chinese, Persian and Aubusson carpets. Even after pine floorboards became common, rugs were often used only on tables, beds and walls. They were too precious to walk on. The earliest type of rugs were functional floor coverings made of rags. These were made from fabric scraps woven together on a loom. Although some rag rugs were dyed one color, most were left natural, resulting in a rug with narrow bands of random color. Few rag rugs remain. They were functional floor coverings, discarded when worn.

For those houses without a loom, braided rugs were a popular alternative. These were rugs made from scraps that were cut into strips, folded and sewn together and then braided in concentric circles until the desired circumference was attained. The individual strips of braid were held together by thread.

Braided rugs are still immensely popular and can give any room a colorful charm. Machine-made copies of colonial patterns are available in many large department stores. You may also be able to unearth braiders who will produce a custom-made rug, but the best way is to do it yourself. Making a

otherwise, the rug will not lie flat. When the desired size is reached, cut off the braid and tuck back the tip of each strand into its tube. Then angle a short segment under the previous row and fasten securely. Encircle the whole rug with a final strip of braid, sewing the ends together before lacing it to the rest of the rug.

Hooked rugs were also a common floor covering. These were sometimes made of rag strips cut half an inch to an inch wide. To make a hooked rug, burlap or loosely woven canvas (the material must be sturdy enough to provide backing yet supple enough to allow a needle to pass through it) was stretched across a standing wooden frame and a design was traced or drawn on the canvas. A hook-shaped needle, like a crochet hook, was punched through the canvas from the front, catching the yarn and drawing it through the hole, leaving a loop of yarn on the surface. Straight rows of even loops gave the rug a smooth surface. Typical designs were stylized flowers, ships and fruit baskets.

braided rug is a simple and fun undertaking, and anyone who understands the rudiments of sewing should be able to do so with no trouble.

The first requirement before starting is to make sure the materials you are going to use are all of the same weight. Wash, dry and then cut each piece of fabric lengthwise into strips two inches wide. Trim the ends of the strips diagonally and sew them together. Select three long strips, fasten the ends with a safety pin and then braid the strips together—left over right, right over left—making sure to keep the plait taut.

Once you have accumulated a store of braids, move to a large table. To begin the rug, cut a six-inch length of braid, tuck the tips of each strip down inside its tube and stitch across the ends, sewing the three strips together. Use carpet thread and a sturdy needle—a curved needle works well. Ring this center strip of braid with succeeding lengths of braid. Each new addition must be secured to the preceding one. Do this by sewing through the outside strand of the last circle of braid and then through the outside strand of the new circle of braid. Bring the needle back through the new braid at an angle and begin a new stitch. Be sure to keep your stitches tight,

BASKETS

If you prefer the utilitarian to the purely aesthetic, baskets may be the logical craft to collect. You can arrange baskets in a corner or use them for substitute vases, laundry hampers or magazine racks. Baskets serve as excellent pots for indoor trees. Like glass and pottery, baskets are one of man's earliest creations. They come in all shapes and moods. Old Shaker baskets can be austerely elegant, Indian baskets wildly colorful. Nantucket lightship baskets, which come in graduated sizes and were woven by sailors on duty on the floating lightship off that Massachusetts port, and are extremely valuable today.

Basket-making materials included anything that was easy to find: bark, yucca, straw, oak, ash, hickory splints, pine needles, cane, cattails, various grains, vines, willow and reeds. Splint was the most prevalent material. To gather it, the basket-maker cut down saplings during winter, when no sap was flowing. After felling, he cut the tree into lengths and soaked it in water. Then the bark was stripped away. The splints were cut with a hand knife to desired lengths and thicknesses. The basket was formed by weaving two sets of splints, the warp and the weft, and binding them at the top with a hand-cut wooden rim.

In 1880, splint-cutting machines were perfected, resulting in an abundance of these distinctive

crosshatched baskets. Splint baskets are rarely decorated and because of their durability, they are often used to hold firewood or laundry.

Willow was also an ideal material for baskets. Like splints, the shoots were cut during the winter and then soaked and peeled. Most willow baskets were given a crosshatch weave and left undecorated. Fishing creels, picnic baskets and trays are traditionally made from willow. Occasionally the baskets will have beaded handles and floral designs.

Sweet grass baskets are made from a wide-stalked plant common to the Northeast and Great Lakes regions. The grass is harvested in the spring and cured over heat until it curls into thin strands for weaving. These baskets are still made by the Chippewa Indians of Michigan, the Penobscot tribes of Maine and the Micmacs of Nova Scotia. The straw of the rye plant is another favorite. The straw is harvested when ripe, then trimmed and soaked in water until the stalks are pliable enough to be twisted into coils. Then the coils are secured to each other with string, thread or grass. Because of this method of construction, straw baskets are limited to round or oval shapes. A few straw baskets are painted, but most are natural, unadorned by handles.

84

COLLECTIBLES

Collectibles—you hear the word everywhere. Pick up a business journal and undoubtedly there will be an article on the investment potential of this or that collectible. Turn on the TV and you find a story about a woman who scours the local garbage dumps for tin cans from the twenties. There is even an encyclopedia—from A to Z—of collectibles. But what exactly are collectibles? Generically, collectibles are anything you choose to collect, be it glass insulators or valentines, but more realistically, collectibles are the antiques of the future. Some, like folk art or quilts, have already become valuable while others are objects whose worth is largely sentimental; anomalies that are either too new or too unusual to be legitimately considered antiques.

The following pages offer a sampling of collectibles. With a little patience and perseverance, most can be found in all parts of the country. Some will be discovered in junkyards, others in old buildings and houses about to be torn down. Still others can be located at flea markets, auctions and estate sales.

Flea markets can provide a valuable introduction to the world of collectibles. Stroll through any large market and you will be staggered by the array of oddities arranged on the tables. Take your time, browse and inquire as to prices. Some will seem outrageous, others bargains. Whenever possible, quiz the collectors on their particular passions. Because most collectibles lack official price guides, collectors are the best repository of current market values. And most of them are excellent oral historians.

Auctions, by definition, are a gamble. It is the auctioneer's job to coax the price as high as it will go. Consequently, auction prices do not necessarily reflect current values. If the auction is well publicized, chances are that the audience will consist of other collectors, and bidding will be stiff. On the other hand, if the auction is held in a rural village, the crowd may consist of interested neighbors, and you could leave laden with bargains. In any case, be sure to arrive early and inspect thor-

oughly all the merchandise. To prepare for an auction, subscribe to auctioneer catalogs and newsletters that will keep you abreast of current prices.

Estate sales are a notch above auctions. These are generally well-publicized affairs boasting a roster of exquisite antiques and an audience of antique dealers and collectors. The value of an estate sale lies in the possibility that, while everyone else is clamoring for the cherry drop-leaf table, you might be the only person bidding on the whirligig.

Are the magazines correct? Will you get rich? Although collectibles such as quilts and folk art are already valuable, future bank vaults will probably not yield abundances of Early American pottery or turn-of-the-century kitchen utensils. Collectibles are a different kind of investment. On the simplest level, they can add a distinctive tone to your country home. Old stoneware crocks, for example, are perfect umbrella holders. Baskets can be filled with pencils and letters and other minutiae of everyday life. An old apple parer can bring a conversational touch to the modern, streamlined kitchen. But an old whirligig or a quilt will also enrich your life in a more profound way: collectibles are pieces of the past that will never be produced again and by collecting them, you will be preserving part of our national heritage.

WICKER

Wicker—a catchall term for woven rattan, reed, dried grass, willow, cane and other pliable materials—has been around almost as long as man himself. The ancient Egyptians made wicker coffins and the Incas fashioned it into boats to sail across Lake Titicaca. But the golden age of wicker began in America in 1855, when a Bostonian named Cyrus Wakefield gave up the grocery business and opened a factory to manufacture wicker furniture. For the next 75 years, wicker was used in every conceivable manner. There were wicker baby carriages, bookcases, rocking chairs, plant stands, settees, davenports, arm chairs and lounges. The Gadabout Motor Company of Newark, New Jersey even offered its customers a wicker automobile.

The earliest wicker shared the Victorian era's infatuation with French Rococo—all flowing curves, scrolls and complicated weaves. The early furniture was handmade and expensive. Settees and diamond-backed rocking chairs were visible on many affluent porches. By the late 1880s, the catalogs of Sears & Roebuck and Montgomery Wards were advertising low-cost copies of the most popular designs. At the same time, wicker moved indoors. Matching living room and dining room sets were readily available. Less common were bookcases, étagères and chests of drawers.

The Victorian style was sup-

planted around 1910, when taste tended more to simplicity. Angular, straight-backed mission furniture was preferred and the overindulgence of late Victorianism came to be considered gauche. Many ornate pieces were carted to the dump or interred in the attic. In 1917, a loom for weaving wicker was perfected, thus allowing for more

complex designs, but effectively ending the age of wicker as a handcrafted commodity. Mechanization enabled wicker to incorporate the art deco styles that characterized the 1920s. The famous diamond design woven into the backs of most Art Deco wicker is one way to identify wicker furniture of the Twenties.

Most collectors prefer the flair of the Victorian period. They look for unusual pieces. Wicker easels (used for displaying paintings), piano stools and the early settees and chairs are all valuable. Matching sets are also treasured. Baby carriages, which were produced in all sizes, shapes and prices, are very collectible. They came as fancy Pullman sleeper coaches, with attached parasols and upholstered interiors, as well as modest park carts and sulkies that were drawn along by handles and came with two wheels instead of four.

When buying wicker, look for pieces produced by the major manufacturers. Aside from Wakefield, wicker was principally made by Heywood Brothers, the American Rattan Company and Lloyd Manufacturing Company. Old wicker pieces are generally heavier and sturdier because they were built with hardwood frames. Later furniture used bamboo. You can gauge the age of the wicker by running your hand over it: old wicker is smooth and thick, newer wicker is thin and slightly fuzzy to the touch. Most 20th-century wicker is made with woven paper. Another sign of age is the weave. The weaving on early pieces is extremely tight. A more open style became popular at the turn of the century, due to labor costs. Much of this wicker is known as resort style and the chaise lounges and chairs are often referred to collectively as "Bar Harbor" pieces.

The ideal finish for wicker is natural, with a light coat of varnish for protection. But most wicker is covered with layers of paint. A commercial stripper can remove the paint, but this may also weaken or dissolve the joints. A safer way to remove paint is to use a toothbrush and a water-soluble chemical solution.

QUILTS

Twenty-five years ago, it was possible to walk into any antique store and find quilts piled on a back shelf or hidden in a cupboard, extravagant and forgotten examples of the creativity that once graced the manufacture of everyday objects. Most were too old and musty to use as blankets, and the idea of hanging them on a wall like a tapestry was considered absurd. Today, quilts are recognized as superb pieces of folk art and are avidly sought.

Simply put, a quilt is a fabric sandwich. It has a top, a middle that is usually cotton batting, raw wool or textile scraps and a backing. The layers are sewn together with quilting stitches. American

quilts use a running stitch, while Europeans favor a backstitch. In the 17th century, plain woolen quilts were a standard in colonial homes and quilting bees were festive respites from daily toil.

Quilts are generally divided into three main groups. First, there is the whole cloth quilt, which is made from two large pieces of fabric, one for the back and one for the front. Whole cloth quilts are rare and do not generate the enthusiasm that collectors feel for

the other main types: piecework and appliqué. Taken together, piecework and appliqué are known as patchwork quilts.

Collectors are clamoring for quilts, and colorful ones like these can be found at flea markets and auctions around the country.

Pieced quilts were the everyday quilts, made from whatever colorful scraps of fabric were available. The scraps were sewn together at the edges to form the top layer of the quilt. These quilts relied on serendipity and some of the abstract designs in a fine pieced quilt are breathtaking. Extreme examples of pieced quilts were the lap robes in vogue in the 1880s and 1890s. These "crazy quilts" were riots of silk brocades, velvet and satin pieced together in all shapes and sizes.

The other major category, appliqué, consists of cutout designs stitched onto a plain background. An alternate method was to appliqué a single design onto a block, which was then stitched to several other blocks to form the top layer. Appliqué quilts often have complex motifs, full of birds, flowers and figures.

Although many of the best quilts are in museums or private collections, there are still enough prizes to warrant a thorough investigation of the antique shops, flea markets and auctions in your area. (It was traditional for a girl to make 12 quilts for her dowry.) Regions that supported religious sects, like the Amish and the Shakers, abound in quilts. In the West, the Indians were noted for their unusual designs. When examining a quilt prior to purchase, concentrate on craftsmanship rather than age—some reproductions have

been artificially aged. Look at the quality of the materials, the patterns and colors used. After 1770, most quilts were made from cotton. Calico, chintz and gingham were popular fabrics. Early quilts are often indigo, with floral patterns. The colors red and green were rare before 1850, but quite common after. Aniline dye were not introduced until the 1870s.

Check the stitching: it should be regular but not too even. Machine-stitching was used on the edges of quilts after 1850, but the designs were always sewn by hand. If the stitching and design look too even and symmetrical, you may be examining the product of a quilt kit which appeared on the market in 1935, utilizing standardized designs and pre-cut fabrics.

A Letter from the Past

The following was taken from a booklet by Joan Lyons, based on a letter written in the early 1920s by Abby Rogers to her granddaughter.

July 26, 1925
Sunday

Dear Grand-daughter Harriet,

... I am going to give you a silk patchwork quilt made by my Mother, your Great-Grand-mother. As I was repairing it today, the wonderful tiny stitches, the gay bits of silk—even the lining, brought my childhood so vividly before me, all its joys and good times (I can't seem to remember any bad times), I thought with the quilt I must tell Harriet all about it and the things that made the good times in those days.

First about the quilt—I can see now the box in which all those bits of silk were kept; the pieces of card-board over which each block must be carefully basted before that over-and-over process, and then those innumerable tiny spools of sewing-silk to be used in the sewing and all so entrancing to my childish eyes. I could not have been more than five years old when my Mother gave me a little block to sew, and you can just imagine what I looked like; a fat, fair haired little girl, on a low stool, taking a stitch and being reassured that it was "all right" before pulling the needle through. The lining is part of a dress I had at that time. Children were dressed very differently then, and not as simple as they are now, 'tho of course I did not wear silk every day. One thing I did have to wear and that was an apron, high in the neck and long in the sleeves—I despised my apron. Before I finish telling you about the quilt I want to explain that the silk pieces were almost all bits of some dress worn by the Rogers or Geers and in re-pairing it I put in pieces of silk from my own trousseau—for I knew you would like me to. Your mother will show you which ones they are.

Now I am going to tell you all about the house where this quilt was made. It was ... a queer old rambling one—a hall, with a twisting stair case to the second floor and on each side a parlor and drawing room; back of it the library and din-ing room ... From the dining room was the "Passage-way" to the kitchen. There my father hung his coat and hat with his gloves inside ... Besides the coat and hats in this passage, there stood a large ice-cooler on a table, and Oh, how often the top was removed to receive a delecta-ble lemon-pie to get ice cold for the noon day dinner. That looms very large in my memory of the "passage." The drawing-room was a very stiff formal room—the walls lined with portraits of the Rogers and Geers, mahogany furniture, a carpet rampant with roses, and the whole room pervaded with a perfectly un-homelike atmo-sphere. It was used only for very special com-pany and the airing and "redding" up the room always created excitement with my two brothers and myself. We knew it meant cakes and pies, nuts and raisins, and everything else good to eat. Another thing I remember about that room, when unused, were the oranges spread on huge trays to keep until, in the natural course of events, they were consumed. My father had the

oranges sent to him in boxes during the winter, for in those days there were no fruit stores in northern New York. Indeed, everything was bought in large quantities—sugar and flour in barrels; coffee in sacks in the green bean, (to be roasted by the cook); hams were smoked in the smoke house, and my wonderful Mother (your mother, Harriet, is like her), superintended the making of the sausages and soft soaps.

In great contrast to the drawing-room was the nursery, a small room with a fire place where the "Home-fires" always burned. Here we lived and had our being. . . . It was in the nursery that we always hung our stockings Xmas eve. Each child had its own nail at that chimney corner— and Santa Claus was then as generous as he now is to you and Buddy—only the gifts were simpler but gave just as much pleasure. But, Oh, how cold those Xmas mornings were, for although there was a hot air furnace, it was stoked with wood and not on its job at the early hour we descended the back stairs to examine our stockings.

The library connecting the front hall with the dining room, was not a pleasant room, but one side was filled with books in a mahogony bookcase with sliding doors . . . Some of these books would seem stupid now to girls "The Household Angel", "The Lost Heiress", etc., but there were beautiful editions of Scott and Cooper, Shakespeare and all the standard poets. We had our own shelf and "Water Babies" was one of my favorites, but "Undine" was always the dearest and best . . .

The dining room was the cheerfulest room in

the house. One side was enclosed in glass and in winter was a miniature green house—rows and rows of shelves with potted plants, and best of all, a large oleander grew in a tub, which in early spring bore lovely pink blossoms. The care of all these plants revolved on the second girl who watered them every morning, and later would give her attention to the cleaning of eight or ten kerosene lamps (no electric light as now) reposing on the mantelpiece . . . Every morning

balanced meal." Mid Victorians ate what and when they wanted to and lived ever happy after.

Perhaps you are tired of hearing about the house—you certainly never would have tired of playing in the garden and back yard ... and best of all the Brook, with the bridge across leading to the croquet ground, carriage house and stables. Oh, that Brook ... Its banks were shaded by willows and large flat stones made fine seats for little girls sewing on their patchwork blocks of a summer afternoon. The stints were never long ones and the croquet ground was close at hand and a waiting companion for a hard fought game ...

When we were tired of the croquet ground there were always the barn and the hayloft. We did not venture into the stables—where my father's fine horses were kept. No automobiles did I ride in then, but there were always comfortable carriages and sleighs, and when I was old enough to drive I had my own horse and phaeton.

In looking back to those early years some of it is hazy and far away, but what is vivid and persistent are the play days by the Brook. I can hear its murmur, the splash of wading feet, feel the warmth of those nice flat stones which made such an excellent seat for a little girl. She is sewing together queer bits of silk, and sewing into them dreams of elves and goblins, of a brook, like this one, turning into a torrent, spreading, spreading up to the castle—into a fountain—into Undine.

That's what the Brook, dear Harriet, meant to your Goggs.

after the breakfast the maid would bring a small wooden keeler (tub) to my Mother—she, still seated at the table, would then wash the cups and saucers and silver. That was part of the breakfast Rite—the other part was the consuming of coffee, beefsteak, creamed potatoes, omelets, hot breads, and in winter Buckwheat cakes!! Cereals were unknown quantities, also a "well

KITCHEN ANTIQUES

The kitchen, at the turn of the century, was a weird and wonderful place, full of sieves and sifters, noodle cutters and pastry crimpers. It should be no surprise that more of today's collectibles come from the kitchen than from any other room. Before electric stoves and appliances simplified cooking routines, preparing food was a serious and time-consuming business. Much native genius was spent perfecting gastronomic gadgets. By 1870, there were 141 different kinds of egg beaters registered with the U.S. Patent Office.

Kitchen collectibles come in such variety that most collectors prefer to collect related objects. Corkscrews, can openers and cork pulls, for example, all have related functions and have been manufactured in various guises for decades. Perhaps the simplest type of corkscrew was a steel wire spiral screw which was attached to an oblong wooden handle. One 1909 variation of this handy gadget was known as the "Walker's Universal Self Puller."

An early example of a can opener was the Sargent-Sprague. It had steel cutting blades housed in narrow metal slots and attached to either a steel or metal handle which rotated the can when cranked. You should be able to find many can openers and corkscrews at low prices.

Also related are the various devices used in preparation of fruit: cherry and raisin seeders, apple parers and peach stoners. The "Rollman" cherry seeder boasted that it could seed 20 quarts in an hour. But by far the most prolific of this group was the apple parer. Apples were a staple of the American diet. They were eaten raw, cooked, dried, stewed, liquified and churned into apple butter. The first patent for a wooden apple parer was granted in 1803. By the end of the century, there were steel parers capable of paring, coring and slicing the apple with one turn of the crank.

Collectors also look for the white enamelware made in the 1920s. Flour sifters and ceramic canisters

bring high prices. Breadboards are another prized item. Some boards, intended for use at the table, had slogans like *The Staff of Life* or *Spare Not, Waste Not* carved on their borders. Wood utensils are another bargain. Wooden spoons and forks are plentiful, as are wooden bowls. More refined are the wooden cookie and butter molds, which often featured a design, a flower or an animal.

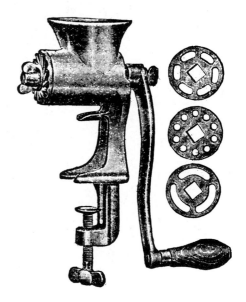

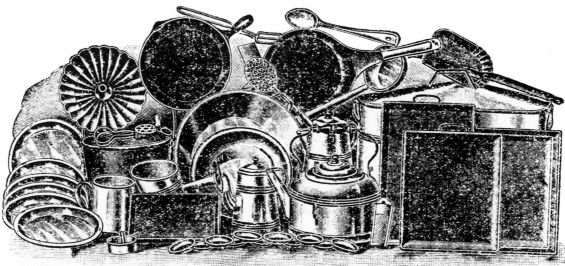

Recently, perhaps as an extension of the bottle craze, canning jars have become popular. Unfortunately it is quite difficult to distinguish between old and new jars. Mason jars have varied little since they were patented in 1858. If you think you have an old Mason jar, look for sheared lips, pontil marks and a keystone design on the glass.

An entire encyclopedia could probably be written about the types of kitchen collectibles. Here is a brief listing of some others to keep an eye out for: biscuit beaters, box graters, coffee and tea pots, trivets (made in many different kinds of materials), salt boxes, jelly presses, rolling pins, doughnut cutters, flour scoops, egg beaters, toasters, waffle irons, all kinds of iron pots and frying pans, churns, cheese graters and step ladders.

Most kitchen collectibles will require some restoration. When cleaning, be sure not to alter the patina as this will destroy the piece's unique character. Both woodenware and tin should be gently washed in warm, soapy water and set outside to dry in the sun. Copper and brass can be cleaned with commercial cleaners. There are also commercial products for aluminum, but the more whimsical may want to try one folk method of cleaning the aluminum by cooking tomatoes or rhubarb in it. The 19th-century housewife also inhibited rust on her iron utensils by applying a paste made of daffodil stalks dipped in red oxide.

94

The whimsical arrangement of antique kitchen implements gives this country kitchen its charm.

Agnes Stables
Work

HOME MADE
PRESERVES
MANUFACTURED BY
H. A. JOHNSON & CO.
BOSTON, MASS.

A large coffee grinder like this one is prized by collectors.

Today you can find as many types of ice cream scoops as there are flavors.

A display of spatterware makes a splash of color against this rough-hewn kitchen wall.

AMERICAN POTTERY

American pottery comes in all styles and sizes. It was produced wherever there was clay and in the 18th and 19th centuries, there were dozens of small manufacturers feeding the American appetite for cheap bowls, mugs, teapots, jugs and plates. We don't have the space to list all the different kinds of pottery, but here are a few that can be found in any antique store or flea market.

Redware: Produced from the red clay common along the Eastern seaboard, redware is the oldest native American pottery. It is usually associated with factories in Pennsylvania, New York and New Jersey, but many other potters produced quantities of this ware. Flower pots, mugs, inkwells, sugar bowls, soap dishes, toys, platters and dishware were made from this distinctive red clay.

Redware was fired at a low temperature and tended to be soft and porous, with a natural reddish brown hue. Various glazes were popular. Many of the simple jugs and jars were coated only on the inside—the potter did not want to waste more of the expensive lead glaze on something so utilitarian. New England potters often added manganese to the glaze to produce a shiny black color. You can also find redware with red, green, brown, black and orange glazes.

The most valuable redware is the sgraffito presentation pieces made by the Pennsylvanian Germans. Sgraffito decoration was applied to pottery by coating an unfired piece with a contrasting color of clay and scratching a design through it to show the color underneath.

Redware has been widely collected since the beginning of this century and pieces like the sgraffito presentation pieces can fetch thousands of dollars.

Stoneware: Until recently, stoneware was spurned by the serious collector, who found it drab and uninteresting, completely lacking color or interesting forms. Today these sturdy crocks and jugs have found many admirers and are readily available to the inexperienced collector.

Stoneware was made from a thick, white clay found in New York, New Jersey and the Mid-Atlantic states. Because of its firing temperature, decoration was limited to blue, black and brown. The ware also resisted molding, so although you may unearth an occasional flask, most stoneware is in the form of crocks and jugs. Decoration was minimal, consisting largely of ships and flowers incised directly onto the wet ware. As the century progressed, free-hand decoration became popular and the pots were adorned with all manner of flora and fauna.

The early crocks were used to store homemade pickles and cookies. The jugs held water or were carried to the barn for the early milking. With the advent of mechanization late in the 19th century, potters began turning out stoneware mixing bowls, pitchers and chamber pots in colors that included white, blue, green and yellow. Though relatively recent, such ware is highly collectible.

Rockingham: Also known as American Brownware, Rockingham pottery is usually associated with the Vermont town of Bennington. But after its appearance at the New York Crystal Palace Exhibition of 1853, dozens of factories began to produce this distinctive tan ware with the brown glaze. Aside from traditional kitchen utensils, Rockingham was molded into such unusual items as Toby Jugs, coachman bottles, Apostle Ware, Rebekah-at-the-Wall teapots, hound-handled pitchers and statuary.

Spongeware: Most collectors are very familiar with this white earthenware, mottled with blue, blue-green and blue-brown, that was produced in the late 19th and early 20th centuries. It was called spongeware because the decoration was applied by dipping a sponge in pigment. It was durable, colorful and simple. All types of kitchen pieces were made from spongeware.

Yellowware: Many of the same manufacturers that produced redware and Rockingham also made yellowware. This was an inexpensive pottery used in mixing bowls, cups, teapots and other kitchen necessities. Decoration was minimal—at most a band of white, brown, black or blue. Such was the utilitarian purpose of yellowware, that few potters bothered to mark their products. Ohio and New Jersey were centers of yellowware production, as was Bennington, Vermont.

Inexpensive and abundant, yellowware is an excellent buy for collectors.

FOLK ART

The word is anathema to most collectors. Art is the domain of museums and people with fat bank accounts. But folk art—loosely defined as objects made for use around the farm and home by people who were untutored in the academic tradition of art—is still being produced and can often be found for a few dollars. Theorem pictures, decoys, whirligigs and toys are all available to the novice collector.

The painting of theorem and mourning pictures was considered a proper occupation for ladies attending the female academies in the 19th century. Mourning pictures commemorated the death of someone close to the artist, or of a prominent figure. Most mourning pictures were done in ink or watercolors, although you can find embroidered ones. A standard conceit was the weeping willow tree, with mourners clustered around a monument bearing the date of death and the name of the deceased. You can find mourning pictures on a variety of materials, among them wood, velvet and glass.

The young ladies of the time also purchased stencils and traced designs onto velvet, silk and wood. These were known as theorem pictures. The best theorem pictures incorporate such individual touches as unusual colors and stylized backgrounds.

You can also find calligraphic drawings, which had their origin in the highly elegant handwriting style invented by Platt Rogers Spence. Most calligraphic drawings are imitations of famous engravings in the strokes of Spencerian penmanship. The artists were usually students who tried with steel pens and colored ink to produce the most exquisite handwriting in their region.

More prosaic than calligraphic drawings and mourning pictures are the Frakturs which German immigrants brought from their native land. These were illuminated manuscripts that recorded the family births, baptisms, marriages and deaths. The name comes from the German typeface on which the lettering was modeled. These colorful geneologies are numerous in Pennsylvania, Virginia, North Carolina, Ohio, Indiana and Texas. They were often stored in the family Bible.

Wood was plentiful in the colonies and after the requirements of daily necessity had been fulfilled, the settler often took out a penknife and whittled toys, rocking horses, farm animals, whirligigs and statues. Two of the better known carvers, both Pennsylvanians, were Wilhelm Schimmel and Aaron Mountz. Both specialized in highly stylized animals that are too unique to be considered toys. Finding a Schimmel or Mountz carving is unlikely, but there are still carvers working in this tradition.

Made by the first settlers, weather vanes were of paramount importance to farmers. The first vanes were handmade in the shape of roosters, horses, cows and other farm animals. By the 19th century, there were many craftsmen producing weather vanes. Hand-hammered copper vanes were made in quantity through the first quarter of this century.

Delicately carved and painted, this pair of harps brings a lyrical touch to an empty corner.

This weathervane is an unusual and comic departure from the roosters, cows and horses that graced most barns.

This copper weathervane, over six galloping feet long, was easily visible to a farmer ploughing in the lower forty.

Craftsmen also made a steady supply of trade signs. To the illiterate, trade signs described pictorially the nature of a particular shop: an apothecary, for example, might be indicated by a mortar and pestle. Pubs were advertised by overflowing steins and bootmakers by wooden shoes.

A piece of folk art that utilized both sculpture and wind was the whirligig. This wind-activated toy was made in many styles. The simplest is an erect human figure with paddle-shaped arms that revolve when the wind blows. On other whirligigs, a cyclist peddles furiously and a washerwoman scrubs her clothes at the slightest breeze. Whirligigs were made of carved and painted wood and gears scavenged from old machinery (which may be completely worn out by now).

Recently, some collectors have begun to collect bird decoys. Decoys were made from all types of wood with the intent of luring game birds down to be shot. The most common decoy was made to float on the water and attract ducks. Another kind of decoy called a stick-up was plunged into the ground in areas where there was little water. The variety of decoys—the most popular were mallards, canvas backs and black ducks—varies depending on the game birds native to a particular area. Decoys are still being made and you should have no problem locating either antique or modern

ones in your area. If you are uncertain of the age of a particular decoy, examine to see if it looks as if it has spent decades being buffeted by wind and wave. Antique decoys have the smooth quality of driftwood. Another clue is the number of coats of paint—most hunters repainted their birds every year. Finally, see if the decoy floats. To the early carvers, function was far more important than form.

CLOCKS AND WATCHES

When we think of clocks, most of us picture the large and expensive grandfather clocks whose movements were regulated by pendulums and weights. More accessible to the novice collector are clocks made between 1880 and 1950. By the end of the 19th century, clockmaking was refined to the point that the clockworks could be housed in a very small case. Major manufacturers like Seth Thomas, New Haven, Ansonia and the Waterbury Clock Company made clocks using tin, brass, iron, stainless steel, glass, marble and plastic. Their designs tended to echo furniture styles popular at the time: you can find clock cases with the flowing lines of art nouveau or the rigid geometrics admired in the art deco period.

Elaborate scenes were painted on the clock face and some clocks had fanciful shapes, resembling churches with sharp gothic spires,

or actual people. Figurine clocks, modeled on personalities like Atilla the Hun or Rubens, were popular, as were the animated clocks popular in the late 1880s and in the 1930s. Movement of the gears caused the figure to perform some action. After Prohibition was repealed, for example, manufacturers produced a clock in the form of a beer drinker who slowly drained his tankard as the hours passed. Equally collectible are musical clocks, cuckoo clocks and the schoolhouse clock.

This pine clock was manufactured by the E. Ingraham Company of Bristol, Connecticut.

Amidst the clutter of a flea market, you can find treasures such as these clocks.

Because of their tiny size, watches presented serious production problems, and for many years they were imported from Europe. Native production began in 1853, but the watches were prohibitively expensive. In 1880, the Waterbury Clock Company marketed a simple watch that sold for only $3.75. A decade later, in 1893, Robert Ingersoll perfected one that sold for $1.00. "The watch that made the dollar famous" was Ingersoll's motto. This heralded a boom in the manufacture of low-cost pocket watches and tens of thousands were produced. Up until the first World War, watches were of the pocket variety only. Wristwatches became popular in the aftermath of the war and gradually replaced the pocket watch as the timepiece of choice. Today, wristwatches are plentiful. Unfortunately, a wristwatch made in the 20s differs little from one manufactured in the 50s.

You can unearth clocks almost anywhere: attics, junk shops, flea markets. Many of these will be inoperable and restoring them could cost you several times the actual purchase price. One hint: if you are serious about collecting clocks or watches, learn something about their works, invest in professional tools and attempt the restoration yourself.

STRIPPED PINE FURNITURE

When America was first settled, pine forests stretched from Georgia to Canada, providing craftsmen with a cheap source of wood. Resourceful builders used this malleable wood to make utilitarian objects for their homes. Its lightness appealed to these pioneers who were always on the go, dreaming of the fertile acres that lay just beyond the next ridge. The spare, functional furniture made in the 18th century and in the first half of the 19th century is known as country-style pine and it is an excellent collectible.

Pine was the wood of the lower and middle classes. The affluent preferred cherry, mahogany and walnut and they imported elaborate furnishings from Europe. Pine was considered rude and inferior. Status-conscious craftsmen often painted their pine to resemble cherry or mahogany. The grains of these exotic woods were carefully duplicated. Such a piece of painted furniture—common in Pennsylvania and other eastern regions—is very valuable in its own right.

You can find pine footstools and benches. Children's chairs were usually made of pine, as were storage boxes. The chest was a ubiquitous piece of pioneer furniture. It was often the only furnishing brought over from the old world. Gradually, with the addition of drawers, the homely chest became the chest of drawers. As native oak disappeared, cabinetmakers turned to pine and a whole range of furnishings were hammered together. Country-style came to an end with the industrial revolution. Mass-produced furniture became the vogue and handmade chairs and tables were consigned to the shed, or the woodpile.

Because of the free flow of articles from America to England, it is difficult to tell precisely when and where a particular piece was made. American carpenters routinely copied English designs. Replicas of popular pieces were reproduced by succeeding generations. When judging a piece of pine furniture, it is best to apply the same criteria as did the makers: is it trim and functional?

To estimate whether a piece is truly old, examine it for wear. Time will cause the edges to wear smooth and soften. Friction will cause the bottom of drawers to wear more in the middle than on the edges. Chain rungs should be scooped out from feet. Chair legs, after decades of pulling and scraping, are rarely even. As wood ages, it acquires a dark tone and takes on character. This is called patina. The patina on each surface should be even.

In restoring a piece of pine furniture, both mechanical and chemical means are available. A hand scraper, sandpaper or an electric sander will work on small pieces. For larger ones, use a chemical solvent, found in any hardware store. Read the directions carefully. After you have bared the wood, you can either apply a coat of shellac or clear varnish, or stain it or apply antiquing paint.

103

104

The Heart Of The House: Wood-Burning Stoves

All across the country, people are rediscovering the allure of wood-burning stoves. Wood-burning stoves draw people to them. Strong, solid and warm, they beckon people to gather round. Who can resist their promise of toasty warmth and comfort? Feeling the radiant heat of a wood-burning stove like the rays of the sun spread over your face and hands is one of the greatest, simplest pleasures known to man. Is it any wonder that wood-burning stoves are being installed all over America?

Not just another pretty face: Webster Stove Foundry combines old-fashioned quality and detailed construction with modern efficiency in their spiral flamepath stove, The Wild Oak.

Unlike heating with oil and gas, heating with wood is a craft. The difference between an automatic heater and a wood-burning stove is like the difference between a motorboat and a sailboat—with one, you merely flip a switch, but with the other, you man the whole operation. Heating with wood is demanding, but it has its distinct advantages.

While gas and oil heat warm the air, wood radiates heat—it actually warms people. A well-tended wood fire puts out a more constant, even heat than a furnace, which switches off and on. Like a fireplace, a wood-burning stove becomes a gathering point for the family (imagine reading bedtime stories in front of the furnace). There is a primitive magic about a fire which lures us to it. Some compare the effect of a fire to that of an opiate—we are mesmerized by the unique colors and perpetual motion of the flame. (According to

105

a character in a Truffaut film, television has seen its enormous popularity because "people seem to want moving images after dinner" and there are no longer enough fireplaces to serve this purpose.) And who can deny that the faint smell of wood burning is infinitely more pleasing than the sickly odor of gas or oil?

The stoves we use today for space heating were preceded by the 18th-century cooking stove. These stoves, which were installed in the keeping room, were much more convenient and practical than cooking fireplaces and they made the keeping room the most comfortable room in the house. Today, stoves provide the same comfort and security for which they were known in the past.

Because fires are perennial sources of warmth and comfort, they never go out of style. We associate fireplaces and wood-burning stoves with times gone by. We can recall the stove or fireplace in our childhood homes—bringing in firewood from the snowy outdoors, nudging the flames with solid iron shovels and tongs and smelling the delightful odor of burning hickory. Think back to the many hours spent reading by the fire, and the countless ghost tales inspired by the fire. There is something about the flames that sets our minds free, that at least for a moment, loosens our grip on the present. Even former president Richard Nixon knew the fascination of a roaring fire. In one of his more benign caprices, Nixon had the air-conditioning equipment in one of the lodges at Camp David made more powerful so that he could enjoy the pleasures of a leaping fire even on the most sweltering summer day.

Before the oil embargo of the early 1970s, wood-burning stoves were rural curiosities, like milking machines and hay balers. But in the past ten years, Americans have rediscovered the plea-

sures of heating with wood. When properly installed and maintained, stoves are safe, economical and efficient. They are solidly constructed to last a long time and are manufactured in an enormous variety of shapes and sizes. Their durability and practicality make them a sound investment for every homeowner.

However, one word of warning. If you are installing a stove yourself, be sure to follow the directions in one of the many books on the subject and then ask your local building inspector to check the installation before you use the stove.

Wood can be a safe and useful supplement to our customary fuels. It is relatively non-polluting and requires less human and mechanical energy to produce and distribute than other fuels. Wood is one of the few renewable sources of energy that we have, and fortunately, Americans have always been blessed with a plentiful supply. With proper woodlot management, our forests can provide us with a never ending source of heat. And while it doesn't make sense for everyone to convert en-

tirely to stove heat, it does make sense to make optimal use of all our sources of energy, including wind, water, solar and wood.

A Dignified Heritage

Some say that fire was given to man by Prometheus. According to the legend, Prometheus and his brother Epimetheus were given responsibility for the creation of mankind. Epimetheus, a bit of a scatterbrained fellow who tended to act on impulse and then change his mind, made man but with his characteristic lack of acumen, gave all the best gifts, including shrewdness, strength, swiftness, fur, feathers, wings and shells to the animals. Poor man was left naked and without protection. Realizing his error, Epimetheus ran to his brother and asked for his help. Prometheus took over, made man upright and brought him fire so that he could protect himself. So great and powerful was his gift that the proud and easily maligned Zeus punished Prometheus for his compassion and wisdom.

Today's stoves have names which bespeak of their venerable heritage. Along with Thor, the pantheon includes Fire King, Defiant, Provider, Majestic, Vigilant, Volcano, Eagle, Hurricane and Glow Master. There is also Aunt Sarah, a stove of unique but no less lofty ancestry.

Fire has always been viewed as a sacred symbol of life. Its magical properties have intrigued kings, philosophers and scientists throughout the ages. In the 6th century B.C., the enlightened Zarathustra reformed the cruel polytheism of Iran and pro-

There's more to the airtight Petit Godin than meets the eye. This compact wood- and coal-burning stove is lined with dense firebrick and the mica window in the fire door allows you to watch the flames and check the fire.

vided for a more beneficent monotheism. Zarathustra dictated that Truth, one son of the new god, would preside over fire, the sole universal and eternal principle. Dour Heraclites, the morose 5th century B.C. philosopher, believed that fire was primal, and the single constant and unchanging element in an otherwise inconstant universe. Heraclites's remarkably precocious notion is the cornerstone of modern physics.

Throughout the ages, fire has been linked with the supernatural and used to invoke unseen forces and drive off malevolent spirits. In some agrarian cultures, it was believed that a cooled, blackened ember secured to the thatch on top of a house or barn would avert lightning bolts for a year. During the Middle Ages, all the old fires of a community were extinguished once a year and formally rekindled with a flame from a new fire. And today, we still burn eternal fires at the feet of monuments and cenotaphs.

But it was not until the 18th century that a Dutch physician named Boerhaave observed that light and heat, the two characteristics of fire, were not precisely co-existent. When fire goes out, the light ceases, but some heat persists. For the first time, it was understood that in order to harness this source of energy man must understand heat.

The stout Webster Oak is assembled by hand and is no less handsome than his younger brother pictured on page 104.

BEN FRANKLIN: THE MODERN PROMETHEUS

It was our own acute observer of fireplaces and smoking chimneys, Ben Franklin, who first invented a stove that provided formidable radiant heat. (Immanuel Kant referred to Franklin as the new Prometheus who had stolen heaven's fire.) A crude quasi-stove known as a *couvrefeu* had been developed during the Middle Ages, but it was nothing like the iron stove developed by Franklin. Franklin's stove incorporated vertical baffles to draw heat from the smoke and flue gases, and because it was set apart from the wall and chimney, radiated more heat into the room. Franklin called his stove the "Pennsylvania Fireplace;" in his characteristically humble style, he refused to patent the stove in his name: "as we enjoy great advantage from the inventions of others, we should be glad of an opportunity to serve others by any invention of ours; and this we should do freely and generously."

Franklin also invented the damper, the movable iron plate within the throat of a chimney used to adjust the draft. Challenged by the saying "as useless as a chimney in summer," Franklin determined to find a way to employ chimneys throughout the year. Because the temperatures inside and outside the house are rarely identical, drafts existed in the chimney that could be put to work. As he wrote:

If the opening be closed by a slight movable frame or two that will let air through, but keep out flies, and another little frame set within the hearth, with hooks on which to hang joints of meat, fowls, etc. wrapt well in wet linen cloths, I am confident that ... the meat would be so cooled by evaporation, carried on continually by means of passing air, that it would keep a week or more in the hottest weather.

This fireplace heater the "Baltimore" was an instant success in 1875 when it was first manufactured by the Boynton Co. of New York.

COUNT RUMFORD

Count Rumford, alias Benjamin Thompson, was the next to try to harness fire as heat. In a paper on the theory and construction of fireplaces published in 1796, the impatient and compulsive inventor outlined his method which he proved would use half the amount of fuel previously consumed, eliminate dangerous drafts and would rarely require the admission of cold air from outside. His sophisticated fireplaces were equally adapted to coal-, wood- or peat-burning fireplaces. Strangely, owing to a quirk in scientific history, Rumford's theories were never absorbed into the main current of fireplace and stove design. Some speculate that his ostracism might have been partially caused by his unconventionality: Rumford was probably the only inventor in history to have

110

dressed, for at least part of his life, completely in white because such clothing is, thermodynamically speaking, the most efficient means of dress.

The Stylish Black Box

Today, stove designers are searching for the new and unconventional. They know that many people with elegant and expensive homes do not want to spoil their decor with an obtrusive or scantily ornamented black box. Today stoves are available in a great variety of styles—everything from antique reproductions to ornate parlor stoves and pot bellies to sleek contemporary models—and in an ever-widening spectrum of colors.

In the 19th century, masonry fireplaces were replaced by iron stoves and fireplaces. Stoves were considered possessions of great pride and beauty. Embossed with stars, pyramids, palms, ferns, fronds, rosettes, scrolls, urns, classically proportioned women, self-help mottoes, cherubs, spears and eagles, they were beautiful representations of efficiency and a visible sign of prosperity.

Soapstone stoves were popular during the 19th century, especially in New England. The stone is easily cut and shaped and occurs in massive dimensions suitable for both hearths and stoves. Because the stone absorbs heat and radiates even after the fire is gone, it is a natural construction material for wood-burning stoves. Many handsome soapstone models are available today.

Sam Jones's Lucifers

Stoves were made even more popular in the 19th century with the invention of matches. Lucifers, the first friction matches to gain broad use, were patented in 1829 by Samuel Jones of London, but their technical development began with Paracelsus, the arrogant and nearly unendurable Swiss physician who isolated phosphorus in about 1526. Because no one in the 16th century knew what to do with the stuff, it was ignored until Hennig Brandt, a German alchemist, used it 128 years later in his attempt to convert silver to gold. Finding phosphorus of no use to him, he sold the secret to a man from Dresden named Johann Krafft. Krafft exhibited samples of the curious substance to a group of scientists in London, where it caught the fancy of an Irish physicist and chemist named Robert Boyle. In 1680, Boyle and a few other entrepreneurial souls started selling fire-making devices that consisted of pleated, phosphorus-treated paper and sulphur splints. But after a couple of sales to the wealthy few who are eternally interested in costly novelties (at the time, phosphorus was more expensive than gold), Boyle's invention was forgotten. Until the ingenious 19th century and Sam Jones, fire was produced mechanically with a flint steel or by friction with a fire drill or grooved stick.

Fortunately, starting a fire is the least of today's stove owners' worries. Wood-burning stoves are models of efficiency and operating one can be a simple and rewarding part of daily life.

This practical, cast-iron wood- and coal-burning parlor stove from Washington Stove Works combines elegance and efficiency. It is made from the casting of the original hand-carved pattern.

Chopping Your Own

An integral part of heating with wood is procuring your own fuel. While it is of course unnecessary for today's stove owner to chop his own wood, it's a lot less expensive that way, and woodcutting is filled with sensuous and kinesthetic satisfaction. Chopping wood delivers a promising reward in return for your time and efforts: there is great satisfaction to be had in chopping a tree to manageable size and seeing it stacked in neat piles for seasoning. Besides, chopping wood is a form of sanctioned violence. As many woodcutters can attest, half an hour's scuffle with an ornery piece of hickory is enough to dispel the most ferocious hostility. The basic steps involved are felling, limbing, bucking and splitting. It does take more strength than golf or pinball, but you don't have to be Hercules to get

the job done. In olden times, woodcutters used to chop with this saying in mind: He who burns wood is twice warmed, when he cuts it and when he burns it.

If you go out to chop your own wood, you will need an axe, a saw and probably a peavey; most modern cutters will also want a chain saw. An axe is a homely and dignified tool, colorless and usually inconspicuous, with an eminent heritage hailing back to primitive man. Axes are all-purpose tools: they can be used for clearing land, building shelter and procuring fuel. A crosscut saw is better than an axe for hardwood trees, and a chain saw, because of its uncommon energy, is probably a worthwhile investment for anyone who has to cut more than a cord or cord and a half. Just be sure to wear ear protectors if you do use a chain saw—they can cause permanent hearing damage.

Hardwoods produce the best firewood, but are of varying splittability. Hickory, oak and maple are probably the most obstinate woods a cutter is likely to come across, with golden birch just behind them. Ash and beech are less stubborn and take the axe with less reservation. Because they sputter, spit, lack durable heat and promote creosote development, softwoods, like pine and fir, are the least desirable fuel woods. But they do split with relative ease and can be used for kindling.

The installation, care and feeding of the wood-burning stove have become for some a subject as obsessional as the newborn baby to its parents. Owners read about stoves, talk passionately to each other about stoves and debate the relative virtues of different makes and models. A word, and total strangers recognize each other instantly as stove owners, that breed apart who belong to the ancient order of fire-worshippers. As the word spreads, and the oil-fired furnace bills grow, more country-living people are joining the order.

Distinguished by their sturdy construction and strong, direct lines, the Cawley 600 and Cawley 400 are decorated with intricate wildlife scenes.

The heavy, deeply rounded structure of the handsome
Cawley 800 ensures overall strength and lasting
durability.

This distinguished and matronly cookstove is the
venerable product of five generations of stove builders
at the Washington Stove Works.

Solid brass gremlins keep watch over this upright,
airtight, thermostatically controlled stove manufactured
by the Thelin-Thompson Co.

Colebrookdale Furnace ten-plate cookstove, c. 1720.
For reproduction sources, see Directory.

These sturdy reproductions (the laundry stove, the Umco and the Victory) are manufactured by Union Manufacturing Co. The laundry stove is similar to a pot-belly, but the top is larger to facilitate boiling large pots of water. Each burns coal or wood. Once advertised for "83 cents and upward" these radiant heaters are still a bargain at $100 to $400.

Country Gardening

The Natural Garden

Today, a new style of gardening is becoming very popular. It is called natural gardening. As with the English Country Garden, this new style takes its inspiration from nature. But rather than uprooting the natural landscape and rearranging it to form a pleasing picture, the natural garden capitalizes on nature's unruly side. The results are less refined—less structured—more like nature itself.

The philosophy of the natural garden is one of collaboration: to control nature not by obliterating it, but by entering into a partnership in which both entities—the gardener being one, and the limitless possibilities in nature being the other—work together. Neither collaborator overshadows the other. The natural garden may appear unkempt, but this tranquil innocence belies the cultivator's expenditure of thought and effort. In fact, the unstructured appearance of the natural garden may be the direct measure of the gardener's artistry.

The gardener combines imagination and inspiration with effort to create a work of art, using nature's living pigments. The gardener intentionally develops a landscape that looks spontaneous and unaffected, not to imitate nature, but to honor it. No one can really improve on the beauty of nature, but the art of successfully modifying the existing components enhances their visibility.

The elements of the natural garden, such as the rolling hills, meandering creek, old apple tree, comely vegetable patch and untended meadow, are visually intensified by the gardener's skill. Through his or her sense of proportion, form and color, nature's gifts fulfill their greatest aesthetic potential.

The desire to involve living things in our lives has never been stronger. But the days of huge private estates (and the gardening staff to maintain them) are gone. No one can afford them. Nor can anyone afford to become a slave to one's hobby. Today, the credo of the natural garden is to get more for less. An understanding of how nature works can give insight into labor-saving techniques. And a selection of material based on low-maintenance plants and plants which look best in their most natural state saves time and effort.

A creek that runs through the natural garden landscape is spanned by a simple wooden footbridge. Familiar house plants such as coleus and gibasis (Tahitian bridal veil) fill in where needed in the dappled shade around and under native shrubs and trees.

Both perennial and annual sunflowers are easy-care musts for the natural flower garden. Their happy faces follow the sun from morning to afternoon, and the seeds attract birds and other wildlife.

This natural gardening philosophy affects every aspect of the garden: the landscape area for beauty and recreation, the vegetable and fruit garden for fresh food, the kitchen herb garden for flavor and fragrance and the areas where wild and cultivated flowering plants grow and bloom for decorating the home and garden. Again, in all these areas, the emphasis is on the selection of plants that look their best in their natural state—unpruned and free—and on the use of plant material that performs over a long period of time with minimum care. Plants may also be called upon to perform double duty. The apple tree produces food but it also puts on a fabulous flower show in the spring, and its gnarled trunk and limbs provide interest throughout the year.

Planning the Natural Garden

Planning a natural garden is largely a matter of selection. You'll have to decide which elements to keep, and which ones to remove. You'll have to eliminate, adjust, readjust, harmonize, synchronize, create and recreate—the tendency may be to create too much. Remember, less is more. Additions must not be made haphazardly.

Take the time to make a leisurely survey of your landscape. Decide which of its existing elements are worth salvaging; specimen trees, meadow areas, natural paths, etc. The natural gardener has to be somewhat clairvoyant, for time is a silent partner in the natural garden partnership. Many plants will take a long time to mature, and your garden concepts may not be fully realized for quite a while.

Soil tests may be needed. In some situations you might have to enrich deficient soils, such as in the vegetable garden, but in most parts of the natural garden, the best solution is to choose plants able to adapt to varying conditions.

Make yourself familiar with climate and moisture extremes. Note areas that remain cold late into spring, and exposed areas that warm earlier. Areas which are too wet or too dry may have to be amended—add drainage material to some, and moisture-retentive material to others—but again, making appropriate plant selections is the natural problem-solver.

In addition to noting topographical features, plant life *in situ* and climatic extremes, observe the path of the sun in the summer, the areas in full sun, the areas in deep shade and the land's relationship to exposure—north, east, south or west. The areas with an unobstructed southern exposure will receive the most sunlight. The vegetable garden should be situated in that area, providing

121

the surface is level and there can be some accommodation for wind protection.

Your success in the natural garden will depend to some extent on trial and error. But gardeners benefit from such experience. The natural gardener learns the principles of horticulture through a remarkable educational process, with nature as the teacher.

Planning the Natural Garden Landscape

When planning the natural garden landscape, let nature be your guide. Start with your notes. Capitalize on the existing features and take advantage of the highlights of the environment, such as level changes, rock outcrops, a stream, natural paths and the like. And begin to consider the merits of your individual landscape's idiosyncrasies and charming distinctions, such as fallen trees and moss-covered rocks.

Accentuate attractive areas, and downplay less-than-perfect ones. Where low levels create moist areas, plant marsh-loving plants. On higher and drier ground, use drought-tolerant plants that enjoy a fast-draining soil. Among the crevices of rock outcrops, plant rock garden plants that will thrive. In these rocky areas, whether natural or man-made, local wild rock plants or hybridized versions will produce results that are as charming as an alpine mountainside.

Natural paths can be enhanced with stepping stones. The paths are instantly transformed into beautiful and useful thoroughfares that retain their natural character and their no-maintenance quality.

In the shade of existing trees, clumps of native ferns and mosses make cool green islands that are virtually self-sufficient. Where shrubs exist, consider adding more; early spring-flowering shrubs can extend the "color season." In areas where the

Cinnamon fern (Osmunda cinnamomea) makes a beautiful ground cover for shady places. Here, under sweet gums and holly, the ferns present a cool vista especially welcome on the hottest days of summer. When choosing ferns to grow in shady areas of your natural garden landscape, investigate the kinds of ferns which grow naturally in the shady, moist areas where you live. Cinnamon ferns will grow in most parts of the United States. Their best feature is that given the conditions they enjoy, they are virtually maintenance-free.

soil is acid (near oaks and evergreens), wild and cultivated blueberry varieties can be grown. If the house has a large south-facing area, deciduous vines, trees or shrubs can be planted to shade the house from strong sun in the summer. These plants shed their leaves in the winter to allow the sun's rays to help heat the house.

Spring-flowering bulbs can be planted in clumps throughout the landscape. This general planting of an area is called "naturalizing." The clumps dot the landscape with color, and the use of old reliables, such as daffodils, insures performance year after year. Refrain from using bizarre bulbs with multicolored flowers—they draw too much small-scale attention, detracting from the overall effect.

Where there are eyesores, many natural solutions are possible. The initial impulse is to hide the problem. A cinder-block pumphouse could be concealed by surrounding the entire building with a hedge of evergreens, but this would look out of place in the natural garden landscape and would cost a great deal. Instead, if you *do* want to employ shrubs, a few large free-form shrubs can be planted directly in the path of the most common sight line—not up against the building, but several feet in front of it so that fewer plants do more concealing. If this solution won't work in your situation, a fast-growing vine can be used. A shaggy one such as Boston ivy will cover a small building in one or two seasons and create a natural camouflage.

Where boundaries must be defined, a sheared hedge is not the natural garden choice. A weathered split-rail fence covered with one ever-blooming vine is a low-cost solution requiring little or no maintenance. If there is a lot of native stone on your property, an assemblage of rocks will make a wall that will last forever.

The forty-nine-cent solution. Problem areas can be hidden with a minimal cash output. This heavenly blue morning glory came from a 49¢ packet of seeds. It's an easy-to-grow vine that forms a quick cover and blooms from July to the first killing frost in the fall. This type of everblooming vine can be most effective when grown for camouflage in a variety of situations. Here, an old picket fence is rejuvenated and softened by this vine. An old dead tree takes on a new life when used as a support for an inexpensive flowering vine. Perennial vines such as Clematis paniculata and trumpet vine (Bignonia radicans) can also be used. Avoid the use of invasive weedy vines such as bittersweet in the north or kudzu in the south. Vines such as these will take over and choke more valuable plants, and are almost impossible to eradicate.

Taming the Wild Flower Garden

The Natural Flower Garden

Flowers in the natural garden bloom from spring to fall. Wild flowers, tried and true annuals and low-maintenance perennials fill the natural garden with color from spring to fall. Flowers needn't be restricted to the formal border; they grow and bloom in all parts of the natural garden landscape: in the vegetable garden, the herb garden, the meadow, the rocky hillside.

A survey of the plants that grow naturally in your area will provide you with an extensive source list for natural garden flowering plants. Take a field guide to wild flowers with you when you go on a wild flower safari. Don't pick! Just write down the names and/or photograph the ones you see. Note the plant families. Next, find cultivars in a good seed catalogue. Chances are

Gomphrena, *the globe amaranth, is an easy-to-grow ever-blooming annual for the natural flower garden. Gomphrenas can be dried for everlasting bouquets. They retain their color indefinitely. For successful garden design, novice garden do well to limit color choices to one or two colors in any one area. Here, purple Gomphrenas contrast delightfully with white ones, making a simple, attractive carpet of color.*

125

Phlox paniculata, *garden phlox, is the wild phlox species from which the familiar perennial hybrid phloxes have been bred. This magenta original has parented a wide variety of hybrid plants in whites, purple-blues, pinks, reds, yellows, oranges and bicolors. Fussy gardeners never allow fancy phlox hybrids to go to seed (form seeds) because the hybrids will always revert to this less desirable original form. However, the natural gardener welcomes this old-fashioned species. Phlox paniculata in this original "vulgar" form is not readily available, but anyone who has allowed phlox to revert will be more than happy to share some of these easy-care and dependable plants.*

Black-eyed Susans have taken over in a small section of this natural flower garden.

126

that these improved varieties with better plant form and bigger and more numerous flowers with longer blooming periods will be just what you want for your garden.

Never transplant wild flowers from the wild. Many of these plants are protected by state law. Most of them do not transplant well, especially when they are in flower. Mail-order companies are offering wild flower plants from seed or as small started plants, an ideal way to get them for your garden.

The least expensive way to have flowering annuals is to grow them from seed. Mail-order seed companies highlight annual flowers that are easy to start from seed and that do well for beginners. Order some of these initially, and keep a diary, noting plants that do well for you. Order more of the plants that have flowered well, and try different varieties of past successes. And always be willing to try something new. But when ordering, don't go overboard. Try to visualize the area you have for flowering annuals, and remember that most seed packets contain 100 seeds. Seed packets provide information on sowing dates and techniques for growing particular annuals. If you've planted something that hasn't come up, or that isn't performing well, replace it with annual plants bought from the garden center.

Natural gardeners are always swapping perennials with neighbors and friends. If you have a day lily that has spread and increased over the last few years, you can dig up extra plants and trade them for some phlox that has done well for your friend. Plants can also be started as cuttings from friends' gardens. Small rooted cuttings make great gifts when you go visiting and your gardening friends will probably reciprocate in kind.

Many people who are tired of the ongoing chore of maintaining a lawn have given over sections of lawn to meadow. The soil in the area merely has to be turned over in early spring by hand with a garden fork, or with a roto-tiller borrowed from a friend or rented from the garden center. Then seeds of native wild flowers are broadcast over the area. Many mail-order catalogues are offering collections of wild flower seeds suitable for your area. These collections contain many different flowers and ornamental grasses and come in varying amounts . . . even by the pound.

A grouping of low-maintenance perennials blooms in the natural flower garden.
Hydrid day lilies share the grouping with bluebird althea (rose of Sharon), and white coneflower (Echinacea purpurea).

The wildflower bouquet in June, July and August. The June bouquet blends wild daisies and wild iris with flowers from woody garden shrubs and trees. The July arrangement features purple loosestrife, a plant that originated in Europe and is now a familiar wild flower in this country.

The August flowers include orange day lilies, Queen Anne's lace (actually a wild carrot) and yellow yarrow (Achillea).

Zinnias, *among the easiest and most dependable summer-flowering annuals to grow, hug the edge of the garden when a physical boundary has been marked the natural garden way—with a split-rail fence.*

Easy-to-grow cosmos *make great cutting flowers for the natural flower garden. Again, simple, complementary colors were chosen to avoid complex color schemes. Cosmos will flower all summer long if the dying flowers are removed regularly. Fading cosmos plants can be renewed by cutting them back by six inches in mid-summer. Cut cosmos seem to arrange themselves when simply dropped into a vase.*

Joe-pye-weed *(Eupatorium purpureum) is a familiar wildflower which grows naturally from Minnesota to New Hampshire and south. Joe-pye-weed should not be picked or transplanted, but should be bought from wildflower suppliers for home-garden use.*

"Carefree Beauty" *is a breakthrough rose. Unlike traditional roses that require spraying and pruning and a great deal of care, "Carefree Beauty" is the first of a new breed of roses perfect for the natural garden. It is nearly maintenance-free, free from disease and produces lovely pink, quality hybrid-tea roses throughout the season. It is self-branching and makes a good choice for a living fence. "Carefree Beauty" also produces colorful, orange-red "hips"—fruits that stay on the plants through the winter.*

Herbs, Fruits and Vegetables: The Self-Sufficient Garden

The Natural Herb Garden

Herbs are among the best plants to grow in the natural garden. They thrive in average soil, and their aromatic properties make them less susceptible to insect damage. And, of course, they are notable for their multiple uses, for flavor, fragrance and garden beautification.

In nutrition-rich soil, herbs produce abundant foliage, but the potency of flavor and fragrance is diminished. They thrive in average, well-drained soil. If the soil is *very* bad in your chosen site, it can be enriched by incorporating well-rotted manure or compost. Spread a three-inch layer over the garden, and turn the soil over to a depth of about 10 to 12 inches. Remove any large rocks. Herbs should be grown in full sun (at least six hours of summer sun each day).

Herbs are seldom attacked by insects, and some actually repel them. However, a few of the annual herbs are pests' favorites. Interplanting garlic and other repelling herbs around the susceptible plants will help. A non-poisonous herb spray can be made from three crushed garlic cloves, or 1/4 cup chopped chives, or hot red peppers or a mixture of all three added to a pint of water in the blender. Strain and add one quarter teaspoon of dish detergent. (The detergent acts as a spreader/sticker, breaking the surface tension so that water doesn't bead up and roll off the leaves.) Place the mixture in a hand-sprayer and spray. This concoction can be used all over the garden and is completely harmless to humans and pets, but be sure to wash all produce before you eat it.

For kitchen use, most people limit their herb-growing to about half a dozen plants. When making a selection, choose herbs that you use most in cooking and the ones that are not readily available in the market. Dill, marjoram, mint, basil, rosemary, chives, sage, summer savory, winter savory, tarragon and thyme are popular choices. For fragrance: lavender, lemon balm, lemon verbena and scented geraniums.

One or two plants of each perennial herb will

Herbs grow not only in the natural herb garden, but throughout the natural garden, and sometimes have rather surprising and creative uses. Here creeping thyme (Thymus praecos) is used as a ground cover in the area of the natural garden landscape where weekend visitors park their cars. As guests arrive, they are greeted by the delightful fragrance released by the cars' tires crushing the plants. The weekly crush doesn't damage the plants. These plants need only an occasional mowing.

be enough for the average family. Perennial herbs become larger each year, so space accordingly. Reserve a larger section of the garden for annual herbs, such as parsley (actually a biennial but usually grown for one season) and basil. Lovers of the great Italian pasta sauce, pesto, believe there can never be enough basil.

Herbs are generally easy to grow from seed, but beginners would be better off starting with small plants from the garden center or nursery. Thwarting weed growth is the ongoing job, and you may have to water occasionally during dry spells. Feed herb plants a balanced fertilizer such as a 20-20-20, but dilute it to one quarter strength to avoid too much foliage production.

Unless you are growing particular herbs, such as lavender, for their flowers, don't allow herb plants to set bud. Flowering reduces the potency of flavor and fragrance, makes plants become spindly and toughens leaves. Keep plants de-budded by pinching flower buds as they appear.

Home herb-preserving is easy. Gather bunches of herbs and tie them by the stems. Place them upside-down in a paper bag, tie the bag shut and hang the bags in a warm, dry place, such as the attic. If the leaves are very fleshy, strip them and set them on a rack or screen stretched over a frame, and place it in a warm, dry place—near a radiator or in the oven with a pilot light, the door left slightly open—for a few days. Then store the completely dried leaves in opaque air-tight containers.

Many people freeze herbs. Parsley and chives freeze especially well. Place the chopped leaves on a sheet of aluminum foil and fold or sprinkle chopped herbs into water-filled ice cube trays and freeze. The herb cubes can be removed from their trays, and stored in plastic bags, to be thawed for individual servings.

Tomatoes star in the natural vegetable garden. They yield the most fruit in the least space, and are easy to grow. Among the tomato choices are: Early Girl, the Patio Prize, a good choice for containers, Roma, Italian plum-type, and the familiar giant, Beefsteak.

Flowering dahlias *share a tiny corner of the natural vegetable garden with a group of assorted vegetable plants, including the attractive rhubarb chard (red stalks, center of photo).*

Principles of the Natural Vegetable Garden

The initial reason for starting a vegetable garden may be economic, a reaction to inflation and spiraling food prices. But the real reward for growing your own fruit and vegetable favorites is the incredible luxury of being able to pick fresh, nutritious produce at the peak of its ripeness and flavor. A head of lettuce grown 3,000 miles away, picked, chilled, shrink-wrapped, shipped and purchased two weeks later, can't compare with the same thing eaten fresh—within an hour of picking. And nothing can compare with the pride one gets from being able to say, "I grew it myself."

Planning for the natural vegetable garden begins in January when the beautiful full-color seed catalogues begin to arrive. Start with a family survey. Interview family members on which fruits and vegetables are favorites. It doesn't pay to grow spinach or rhubarb if no one will eat it. Also note vegetables and fruits that are difficult to come by or are too expensive. The tendency when ordering seeds is to buy too many. Draw a plan of your natural vegetable garden and visualize plants as they will look at maturity to allow for space. Arrange short plants on the south end of the garden, and tall ones in the back, so that tall plants won't shade shorter ones.

Gooseberries are old-fashioned fruits perfect for the natural garden. Easy-to-grow shrubs produce a bounty of fruits for pies and preserves.

Consider how much work you are willing to do, and how much time you'll be able to devote to it. If this isn't your first year of gardening in the vegetable patch, you'll be aware of plants that did well for you in the past. Re-order seeds of past successes, and try new varieties of these plants. Also try at least one new vegetable you've never grown before. You never know what might become a family favorite.

Fruits in the natural garden are grown from nursery stock—either from the garden center or from mail-order suppliers. To reduce the necessity for spraying, always choose varieties that are resistant to plant viruses and diseases. The supplier will be able to tell you. To deal with crawling in-

sects, non-poisonous bacterial sprays are available. Also, hormone-based traps are on the market for other problem pests. A home-made bug spray can be made, following instructions in the natural herb garden section.

The soil in the vegetable garden, unlike other areas of the natural garden, must be enriched. Each fall, a layer of nutritive humus such as compost, decomposed manure or a green manure—a cover crop of nitrogen-rich living plants such as buckwheat, which are sown in early fall after vegetable harvest—is spread on the garden. In late fall or early spring, the layer is incorporated into the soil by turning the soil over and under to a depth of about 12 inches.

Another popular new squash is vegetable spaghetti. The unusual fruits are boiled for 20 minutes for a spaghetti-like dish from the stringy insides of the squash. It can be served with butter and cheese or smothered in sauce for a low-calorie meal. The beautiful vine happily hugs the vegetable garden fence and softens this necessary boundary.

Summer squash and zucchini are easy-to-grow vegetables which long ago established their place in the natural vegetable garden. Squash bears harvestable fruits in as little as 50 days after being set in the garden. This hyprid squash (Gourmet globe) can be eaten fresh in salads, steamed or fried or stuffed and baked. Many new squash varieties, such as Gourmet globe, are bush-type. Instead of having long-rambling vines, these bush-types grow from a central point and form compact plants that are easy to grow and take up less room.

137

Pinecones can be recycled for an extremely attractive garden mulch. The mulch keeps in soil moisture, reduces chances of damage from temperature extremes and discourages weeds. This mulch is being used between creeping junipers, which are popular care-free ground covers for sloping areas where erosion is a problem.

Rough-hewn tree trunks and branches make a formal herb garden trellis with rustic charm. This structure provides a tall visual element among the low-growing herbs, and even though its design is simple, it adds interest to the scene.

Whenever watering the natural vegetable garden, water deeply. Using more water, less often, will make roots grow deep and the plants will be less susceptible to drought damage. General light watering causes roots to grow close to the soil surface which necessitates frequent watering, and increases the possibility of complete crop failure if daily watering is missed.

A moisture-saver, especially useful for the weekend gardener, is easily fabricated from empty plastic gallon containers. Poke some holes in the bottom of the containers, and bury them in the vegetable garden every four feet. Instead of watering the surface of the entire garden, fill the containers. The water is delivered to the roots where it is best used by the plants, and moisture loss through surface evaporation is minimized. Water-soluble fertilizers can also be applied this way.

Mulches are also moisture- and labor-savers. Without mulches, watering would have to be done more often, weeding would be a constant occupation and heat and cold extremes would cause serious damage. One might consider an inorganic mulch; experimentation with black plastic film (polyethylene which comes on a roll and is inexpensive) has found it to be one of the best mulches. The plastic is spread out over the vegetable garden and secured with stones or wooden stakes or by a covering of soil. Holes are poked in

What appears to be a hodge-podge vegetable patch is actually a carefully planned garden designed for successful growth and harvest. Tall Jerusalem artichokes grow at the north end so that they won't cast shadows on other sun-loving plants. The familiar lush green squash plants form a natural border in the southeast corner.

the mulch for vegetable plant seedlings. If you object to the look, the mulch can be made more attractive by covering it with an organic mulching material. Some gardeners prefer to use a mulching cover which can be incorporated into the soil at season's end, such as salt marsh hay, peat moss or bagasse (chopped sugar cane). A two- to three-inch layer spread over the entire garden before planting will serve the purpose.

Organic mulch can be added to the compost pile along with almost all waste from the natural garden. A healthy soil depends on a great deal of organic matter. And making your own compost is a no-cost method for obtaining this soil-enriching material. All organic material can be composted except perennial weeds, which may infect the pile with seeds that will later create weeds in the garden, diseased plant material or any material that may have been treated with poisons or growth inhibitors.

The easiest kind of compost system to employ is the compost pile. Here, one adds organic material to the heap at the top, and removes rich compost from the bottom. The compost pile should be located in a secluded part of the natural garden landscape—reserve conspicuous areas for attractive plantings. A properly made and maintained compost heap, one that is aerated, will not be a slimy, smelly mess.

If you are depositing a lot of soft, wet plant material, such as grass clippings on the pile, it may be necessary to incorporate a coarser, drier material, such as straw, which will allow air to penetrate the heap. Wood chips, sawdust and other woody materials can also be used in the pile, but they should not be a major ingredient because wood robs the pile of nitrogen as it decomposes. The process from one new organic material to rich garden compost takes about two years, but once you get started, you will have a continuous supply of humus. Composting accelerators are

In keeping with the natural garden philosophy, some delicious and unusual vegetables are grown, not only for their food value, but also as ornamentals. This purple cauliflower is one example of a vegetable that is as lovely to look at as a bouquet of flowers. It decorates the fall harvest table and is enjoyed as a side dish. Other particularly attractive plants which make edible garden ornamentals are (to name but a few): Brussels sprouts, which look like small palm trees studded with little cabbages, rhubarb chard, which has brilliant ruby-colored stalks and pepper sweet banana, which has lovely long yellow fruits.

available from garden suppliers to speed up the process.

It will also be necessary to feed the vegetable garden. The simplest way to add fertilizer is with a commercial fertilizing preparation. Preparations are either water soluble for liquid application, or granular, to be dug into the soil. Generally the vegetable garden gets a dose of a fertilizer with a high phosphorus content, but this is a good time to become familiar with the other elements necessary for plant growth. All plant foods have a number ratio that applies to their nutritive content. Numbers such as 5-10-5, 20-20-20 and 23-19-17 stand for the three major elements—always presented alphabetically—in plant food. These are nitrogen, phosphorus and potassium (sometimes in the form of potassium hydroxide or potash). The plant foods also include trace elements and inert ingredients, listed on the container but not included in the ratio.

The three elements affect plant growth in different ways. Nitrogen produces foliage growth. A fertilizer that is high in nitrogen is good for plants which are grown primarily for their foliage, such as grass, evergreens and leafy vegetables such as lettuce. Organic sources for nitrogen are fish emulsion, dried blood, manure, cottonseed meal and—believe it or not—lightning.

Phosphorus promotes sturdy growth and is essential for flower, fruit and seed development. A fertilizer with a high middle number such as a 15-30-15 is used for fruiting food crops such as apples, squash and tomatoes, and for all plants which are grown for their flowers. Organic sources for phosphorus are bone meal and rock phosphate.

Potassium is used by plants in the production of starches and sugars. It is necessary for good root development and for plants that grow tubers, such as potatoes. Potassium also aids in disease resistance. Wood ash is the primary organic source for potassium.

The natural vegetable garden is a constant source of good food for the home, of pride for its cultivator. Through preserving methods—canning, drying and freezing—you can have fruits and vegetables throughout the year.

Annual asters and gomphrena make a pretty picnic arrangement in the shadow of the raspberry patch. Cultivated raspberries are surprisingly easy to grow. The reason that they command such a high price in the market is that they have to be picked when ripe and the soft fruits are very difficult to ship.

Some new cultivated varieties of raspberries are called ever-bearing. These don't bear continuously through the season, but they do bear twice, as opposed to standard varieties that only bear once a season. This natural garden raspberry choice is "Heritage ever-bearing."

Seed Sources

Applewood Seed Company, 833 Parfet Street, Lakewood, CO 80215. Wild flower and house plant seeds. Catalogue—Free

Armstrong Nurseries, Inc., Box 4060, Ontario, CA 91761. Fruit Trees. Catalogue—Free

Bluestone Perennials, 7211 Middle Ridge Rd., Madison, OH 44057. Extensive selection of perennials. Catalogue—Free

Burpee Seed Company, Warminster, PA 18991; Clinton, IA 52732. Complete selection of flower and vegetable seed house plants, bulbs, fruit trees, shrubs, vines, supplies. Catalogue—Free

Comstock, Ferre, and Co., 263 Main St., Wethersfield, CT 06109. Vegetable, herb, and flower seed. Catalogue—Free

Henry Field Seed and Nursery, 407 Sycamore, Shenandoah, IA 51602. Vegetable and flower seed, perennials, house plants, supplies. Catalogue—Free

Green Horizons, 500 Thompson Drive, Kerrville, TX 78028. Source for wild flower seeds.

Greene Herb Gardens, Greene, RI 02827. Herb seed. Price List—25¢.

Gurney Seed and Nursery Co., Yankton, SD 57079. Bulbs, vegetable and flower seed, shrubs, trees, fruits, nut trees, house plants, supplies. Catalogue—Free

Joseph Harris and Co., Inc., Moreton Farm, 3760 Buffalo Rd. Rochester, NY 14624. Vegetable, flower and tree seed. Catalogue—Free

Herbst Brothers Seedsmen, 1000 North Main St., Brewster, NY 10509. Vegetable, tree seed. Catalogue—Free

Kelly Brothers Nurseries, 23 Maple St., Dansville, NY 14437. Vegetable seed, bulbs, fruit trees, shrubs, berries, grapes, roses, evergreens. Catalogue—Free

Lamb Nurseries, E. 101 Sharp Ave., Spokane, WA 99202.

Merry Gardens, Camden, ME 04843. Rare indoor plants. Catalogue—$1.25

J.E. Miller Nurseries, Inc., Canadaigua, NY 14424. Fruit trees and berries. Catalogue—Free

New York State Fruit Testing Cooperative Association, Geneva, NY 14456. Fruit trees. Catalogue—Free

L.L. Olds Seed Co., PO Box 7790, Madison, WI 53707. Vegetable and flower seed. Catalogue—Free

George W. Park Seed Co., Box 31, Greenwood, SC 29647. Flower and vegetable seed. Catalogue—Free

R.H. Shumway Seedsman, 628 Cedar St., Rockford, IL 61101. Vegetable and flower seeds. Catalogue—Free

Springhill Nurseries 110 W. Elm St., Tipp City, OH 45366. Perennials. Catalogue—Free

Spruce Brook Nursery, Rte. 118, P.O. Box 925, Litchfield, CT 06759. Perennials, rare plants.

Stark Brothers Nurseries and Orchards, Louisiana, MO 63353. Fruit and nut trees, bulbs, roses. Catalogue—Free

Stokes Seeds, Box 548. 737 Main St., Buffalo, NY 14240. Vegetable and flower seed. Catalogue—Free

Thompson and Morgan, Box 100, Farmingdale, NJ 07727. European flower and vegetable seed, unusual garden products. Catalogue—Free

Wayside Gardens, Hodges, SC 29695. Excellent selection of bulbs, flowering trees and shrubs. Catalogue—$1.00.

White Flower Farm, Litchfield, CT 06759. Informative catalogue—$5.00

Country Property

horeau moved to Walden Pond because he wanted to live "a primitive and frontier life, although in the midst of outward civilization." In other words, he wanted the mystery of the woods and wildlife, without having to sacrifice the conviviality of such friends as Ralph Waldo Emerson. Before you invest time and money in a country home, you would be wise to be equally candid. Forget, for a moment, the images of sprawling farmhouses and beach cottages that most of us picture when we think of living in the country, and consider just exactly what kind of country you would like to inhabit.

For example, if you are planning to purchase a second home, then travel time will be a prime consideration. Decide how many hours are reasonable and translate that

147

are there? Who takes care of the roads? It is important to remember that the dirt road which is so picturesque during the summer can often be impassable during the winter and the spring. Ask about the zoning laws and find out if the area is being rapidly developed. This could increase the value of any property you purchase, but it can also mean that the rural values that attracted you in the first place may be disappearing. A thorough investigation is never time wasted.

Financing: What You Should Know

Once you've decided where to look, it is time to assess your finances. Obtaining financing varies with the property and the location. If you plan on constructing a new house, keep in mind that most banks will refuse to grant construction loans until any outstanding debt on the land itself is erased. If the house is a second home, then most banks will require a large down payment in cash—usually anywhere from 25% to 40% of the total purchase price. With interest rates soaring, banks are tightening up on mortgages and you may have a difficult time obtaining one for a second home. One alternative: make payments directly to the seller if he is amenable. Again, you will have to make an initial down payment and the length of payment time is usually shorter than the 20- to 30-year bank mortgage. The interest rate is likely to be the same as at a bank, but this is negotiable.

With all this in mind, draw up a financial plan that answers these three questions:

1. How much of your own money do you wish to spend?

2. How much money do you wish to borrow?

3. How much money can you afford to pay monthly, quarterly or annually?

Then go see a banker in the area. Bankers serve as a source of money, loans and advice. A banker can tell you about the local financing situation and what local source has money available at the most reasonable rates.

figure into miles. Then take a map and, placing a compass on the place where you now live, draw a circle using the agreed-upon distance as the radius. This is the area in which to search.

Another important consideration is recreation. Ask yourself whether the area has mountains and lakes, skiing and swimming. Are there golf and tennis courts nearby? A movie theatre?

If you are planning a permanent relocation, you will want to investigate the tax rate and the type of local government in the area that attracts you. What sort of utilities

148

Where To Look

The obvious source of available property is a real estate agent. A reputable, efficient realtor—one who belongs to the National Association of Realtors and subscribes to its strict code of ethics—can be immeasurably valuable. Although agents receive their commission from the seller, they are naturally interested in a smooth transfer. National operations, such as Strout Realty, United Farm Agency and Century 21, are good bets, as are local real estate agents. A good one often has an entree at the local banks.

Also useful are newspapers that serve the area you are investigating. Often, these properties are not listed with any one agency and it may be possible to deal directly with the owner. This is the case when a listing calls for the "principals only."

Old or New

The agent will probably show you a variety of houses, some of them farmhouses with 15 rooms, others in developments or condominiums. This brings up the problem of old or new. Old country places can have a captivating character and in some cases a new coat of paint and a few minor repairs will re-

store them to mint condition. More often, older houses require some renovation. The plumbing may be as old as the giant maple which shades the driveway.

When buying an older home, it is a good idea to seek the advice of a professional engineer, employed by a building inspection service, to conduct an impartial survey of the overall structure, the foundations, the roof, the pipes, the electrical wiring and the insulation. If an engineer is not available, an architect or a reputable builder can perform the inspection. Should you decide to inspect the house yourself, here are some guidelines:

Exterior Areas: Check all walls, siding, roof and windows. Test the window caulking. If there are storm windows, check those as well.

Termites: Jab an awl or any other sharp instrument into the supporting wood beams. If the awl goes in easily, you may have trouble. However, dry rot and termites can be remedied. Call a local exterminating company to do a thorough inspection.

Water: Go down to the basement and look for seepage. Are there puddles of water or evidence of moisture on the floor? Look for cracks in upstairs walls and brown stains on the ceiling. Look for black carpenter ants. These insects are attracted to moisture. If you find them, then almost definitely you have a leakage problem.

Electrical: Examine the electric meter and the fuse box. Check the location of switches, outlets and fixtures. Are they old-fashioned? Old-fashioned switches and fixtures may be quaint, but they can also be hazardous. Many old buildings were wired with aluminum wire, now known to cause fires. If you have any questions about the wiring, have a professional check it out.

Heat: What sort of heating system is there: electric, gas, oil? Ask to see current, especially winter, bills. Large, drafty houses built when energy was plentiful may be prohibitively expensive to heat on a year-round basis today.

Plumbing: What sort of sewage system is there: cesspool, septic tank, or publically managed? Find out when the pool or tank was installed and when it was last cleaned. Replacement or cleaning can be expensive. If water is drawn from a well, check the well. The amount of water you will get can be gauged by the diameter of the well but there can be seasonal variations, so make a point of inquiring about these. Flush the toilets and run the faucets. If the water pressure is not sufficient, you may be faced with a costly redrilling of the well.

kitchen shelf or the exact location of those ceiling spots in the dining area. Being present may make you feel like a nuisance, but it is the one way to insure that the house you visualized is the one you get. Besides, you are the ultimate boss. You are paying the bills.

Up until a few years ago, building your own house was a case of *caveat emptor*—buyer beware. Now that has changed. The national Association of Homeowners Warranty (HOW) program provides protection against major structural defects on new houses for up to ten years. You, as buyer, and your builder both sign an agreement in which the builder agrees to fix, in the first year of occupancy, all defects caused by faulty workmanship and materials at variance with HOW standards. For the second year of coverage, the insured warranty continues to protect against defects in the electrical, plumbing, heating and cooling systems, as well as any problems with the building's overall structure. For years three through ten following completion of the house, the insurance carrier directly insures the buyer against structural defects.

The intent of HOW is to give the builder two years to correct his mistakes or lose HOW accreditation. Then the responsibility is transferred to HOW's insurance carrier. Such programs as these not only protect the owner but should help to improve the quality of home construction.

With these guidelines, you are ready to assess that old house and decide either to buy or pass it up.

If you are buying a new house that was built within the last few years, follow the same procedure as with the old house. Building practices vary widely and many new houses have serious flaws.

If you plan on building a new house, then the success of your project will largely depend on the expertise of the builder or general contractor that you hire. Once your architect has drawn up an acceptable design, submit the plan to several contractors for bids. Then

check out their reputations with former customers. Ask if they met their timetable, their estimates. Was their work of acceptable quality? Is their credit good with the bank and the lumberyard? Once you have this information, you should be able to make an intelligent choice.

If possible, try to be on hand while the house is being built or at least visit the site from week to week. Many contractors have several jobs going at once and the final details of your house may be in the hands of someone who is a trifle hazy about the height of a

157

Resort Condominiums and Developments

Because of their popularity, a word should be said on the subject of buying property in developments. Developments are designed with convenience and recreation firmly in mind, making them attractive purchases for many people. The developer provides water, electricity and sewage disposal. Before buying a condominium or development house, thoroughly investigate the background of the sponsors. Learn how the administration of the development is structured and

how it seems to be working out—not all are adequately financed or well managed. Find out what kinds of people live in the development. Who your neighbors are matters. If you are purchasing the house or condominium as a future investment, don't expect its value to rise appreciably until all the units in the development have been sold.

Building Your Own

The ultimate option—and one chosen by an increasing number of country dwellers—is to build the

house yourself, using one of the many kits available on the market. House kits are not new. The frames of early New England homes were shaped and fitted by a local joiner who stamped each beam with a Roman numeral indicating its position in the total structure.

Modern kits come in a variety of styles and various stages of development in the finished product. Some provide modular units already equipped with plumbing, wiring and carpeting. The assembling of these is fairly simple, and in a matter of days you can move in. Other kits consist of little more than pre-cut lumber and a set of

a house kit is to decide what sort of a house you want. Then shop around. For a nominal fee, most manufacturers will provide you with literature on the kits they sell. Know what the kit includes and what you must provide. Does the kit come with a heating system, plumbing, electricity, septic system, well and foundation materials? Or will you have to provide these, at considerable extra expense? Are you allowed substitutions—a different heating system, for example? What are the shipping costs?

When the kit arrives, check to see that all the materials are there, then examine them for quality. Is the lumber dry or green? Is it warped, or does it show signs of dry rot? Are there large knots or other structural flaws in the framing timbers? Do the doors and windows seem to be cut true and to fit without any signs of warping? If not, speak up now and avoid future headaches, and high heating bills if you live in a cold climate.

There are many reasons to buy a kit home. It is cheaper than hiring a general contractor and theoretically it should take less time to complete. But the real reason to invest in a kit is the satisfaction that comes from fashioning a house with your own hands. So give yourself enough time to do a good job. If you do, then you should end up with a tight, level and durable structure that you'll be happy to call home.

detailed instructions. They require more time and expertise. Kits that reproduce the post and beam construction of the early New England home are popular. A good source of listings for house kits is the 112-page *Guide to Manufactured Homes* (published by the National Association of Home Manufacturers, 6521 Arlington Boulevard, Falls Church, Virginia 22042).

The first step before investing in

The 1770 House in East Hampton, New York provides old-fashioned comfort to overnight visitors.

Country Inns: Then and Now

Perhaps you haven't quite decided whether you want to make a commitment to country living. Or perhaps you're already searching for that perfect piece of country property. In either case, an overnight stop at an old staging inn is a unique experience which can put you in a country frame of mind.

The earliest Inns, called Ordinaries, were considered so vital to the social life of the colonies that the Massachusetts General Court passed a law penalizing any town that failed to provide this convenience. Although these Ordinaries provided the occasional traveler with rest and food, a more common customer was the churchgoer who journeyed miles to attend the marathon sermons of the day. Between the morning and afternoon sessions, it was customary to repair to the Inn to discuss local events while imbibing beer, ale or cider. The bar was the center of local gossip. Here the town newspaper was kept, read and reread. Political issues were debated and travelers were pumped for stories and news of other areas.

For the traveler, the accommodations were rude but welcome after a day's journey on the bridle paths and Indian trails that connected the villages of 17th-century America. Everyone, regardless of sex, slept by the fireplace. Coats doubled as pillows. In the morning, after a cold wash at an outdoor basin, a breakfast was served that might consist of leftovers from the previous night's meal, johnnycake and cider. Johnnycake—made from cornmeal flour and water and baked on a shingle in the fireplace—was a dietary staple. Coffee was unknown, as were forks. Fingers and knives were the usual utensils.

The 18th century saw increased travel and improved roads, prompting the Inns to concentrate on creature comforts. By 1773, stage lines were operating between New York and Philadelphia and a decade later, regular lines connected New York to Boston and Albany. The journey from New York to Albany lasted three days during the summer and four or more in winter. A typical day lasted from five in the morning until 10 at night. Josiah Quincy, who traveled from New York to Boston at about this time, wrote that the "carriages were old and shackling, and much of the harness made of rope. One pair of horses carried the stage 18 miles. We generally reached our resting place for the night, if no accident intervened, at ten o'clock, and after a frugal supper went to bed, with a notice that we should be called at 3 in the morning, which generally proved to be half past two."

If you were traveling by horse or stage, you were alerted to the presence of an Inn by an elaborate sign, undoubtedly the creation of one of the itinerant painters who wandered the colonies executing murals. Since most people were still illiterate, the signs tended to be strongly pictorial. The Red Lion and the Golden Bull were two popular names for Inns. After the Revolution, a number of George Washington Inns appeared.

The Inn, as the stage approached, usually appeared as a solid white building surrounded by outbuildings. There would be a stable, a coach house, storage sheds, ice house and a woodlot filled with neatly stacked cords of wood. Further off would be the farm buildings, which provided the guests with fresh produce. Most Inns had a chicken house for fresh eggs, a piggery for pork and a corn crib and cowshed.

There was rarely any landscaping aside from the lilac and rose bushes that grew naturally. To one side of the entrance was a garden filled with vegetables and herbs. At the door you were greeted by the Innkeeper, who functioned as the community greeter and factotum. This genial host knew everyone in the community and often parlayed this intelligence into political office. Innkeepers often served as selectmen, road commissioners, tax assessors, tax collectors or town moderators. Occasionally they held all these offices at once. James Fenimore Cooper spent several months roaming the countryside with Lafayette in 1824. Naturally, Inns were an important part of their itinerary, and Cooper felt compelled to contrast the young Republic's Innkeepers with those of England: "The Innkeeper of Old England and the Innkeeper of New England form the very extremes of their class. The former is obsequious to the rich; the other unmoved and often apparently cold. The first seems to calculate at a glance the amount of profit you are likely to leave behind you, while his opposite appears to calculate only in what manner he can most contribute to your comfort without materially impairing his own."

Once inside the Inn, most travelers headed immediately for the bar, which was liberally stocked with beer, ale, wine, rum and cider. Most stood at the broad counter, but there were small tables and, perhaps in a far corner, a Windsor chair with a writing arm. The meals, much improved since the last century, depended upon what was available. Some Inns were noted for certain dishes. The

Mendenhall Ferry Tavern, near Philadelphia, was widely touted for its catfish suppers. In 1790, Henry Wamsey, an English clothier, dined at Captain Flagg's Inn at Weston, Connecticut, and was served a breakfast of beef steaks, veal cutlets, coffee, bacon and eggs, toast and butter.

If any part of the Inn remained crude, it was the sleeping quarters. Sarah Knight, an inveterate traveler who later opened her own Inn in Connecticut, described a night in Rye, New York like this: "arriving at my Apartment I found it to be a little Leanto Chamber furnisht amongst other rubbish with a High Bedd, and a Low one, a Long Table, a Bench and a Bottomless Chair." Needless to say, the bed was hard, the quilts insubstantial, and Sarah groaned the night away.

By the 1800s, with the Revolution won and with the Industrial Age on the horizon, Inns became less like temporary bivouacs and more like the hotels of today. In a contemporary journal, entitled *Reminiscences of a Hotel Man,* the typical Inn was described as averaging twenty-five rooms. It was painted white with green blinds and trim and it offered a public parlor, a dining room and a bar with a fireplace big enough to burn a cord of wood.

The menus, which were printed on long, narrow strips of poor paper, were extensive. In 1851, the American House in Springfield, Massachusetts, offered guests a choice of mock-turtle soup; boiled bluefish with oyster sauce; boiled chickens with oyster sauce; boiled mutton with caper sauce; boiled tongue, ham, corned beef and cabbage; boiled chicken with pork; roast beef, lamb, chickens, veal, pork, and turkey; roast partridge; fricaseed chicken; oyster patties, chick pie, boiled rice, macaroni, apple, squash, mince, custard, and peach pies; boiled custard; blanc mange, tapioca pudding, peaches, nuts and raisins.

The wine lists were also broad. An 1840 list included Mumm's champagne, for two dollars; the best Sauterne, at a dollar a quart; Rudesheimer 1811, and Hockheimer, two dollars; clarets, Burgundies and Madeiras were more expensive; Constantia (twenty years in glass) and Diploma (forty years in wood) were six dollars a bottle.

Today's country Inns are part of our national heritage. They are renowned for their pastoral settings, elegant food and comfortably appointed rooms, many of which include feather pillows and pieced quilts. The 1770 House, on the main street of East Hampton, Long Island, New York is an exquisite example of how far the Inn has come since the early days of communal sleeping and johnny-cake.

Surrounded by a picket fence, the 1770 House is a graceful colonial that in the past has been a general store, a private home, a dining hall for the students of Clinton Academy, once the oldest academy in the state, a boarding house and a public Inn. It experienced something of a heyday in the 1940s and 50s, when it drew its clientele from show business, particularly those actors appearing at the John Drew Theater across the street. But by the late '60s, the place had fallen into disrepair.

It was then that Sidney and Miriam Perle, who had been shopping around for a small Inn for some time, fell in love with the place and decided to fix it up. They spent months scraping and painting and patching. They pumped over a foot of water from the basement and repaired the plumbing. Then they filled the rejuvenated rooms with an extensive collection of mid- to late-19-century antiques, with a special emphasis on clocks.

Whereas the bar was once the heart of the earlier Inns, the dining room is now the central room of the 1770 House. The dining room combines chocolate walls with white trim. The chairs are bamboo with a Regency design. Near the bay window hangs a stained glass panel of a pre-Raphaelite maiden. On each table, a shaving mug is filled with fresh flowers.

168

Since Miriam Perle once ran a cooking school and catering service, the food is an eclectic mix. Guests can dine on puffed crêpes and honey butter; blintzes florentine; poached salmon with sour cream and dill; soup pistou; and rack of lamb persille, among other dishes. After dinner, guests retire to the taproom where, during the winter months, a fire burns on the 18th-century hearth. Here you can sip on a post-prandial cup of grog and nibble slices of apple brown betty, topped with marzipan, or the Inn's famous whiskey cake.

The Inn's delicate whiskey cake is served in this warmly lit taproom.

The comfortable and handsomely appointed sitting room of the 1770 House, replete with 19th-century antiques, invites conversation.

Every bedroom in the 1770 House is handsomely decorated with original antiques and quality reproductions.

It is here, in the sun-filled dining room, that Miriam Perle serves her savory continental and American specialties.

Country Directory

 he following section is what you might call an "Annotated Attic." A catchall of information to satisfy the rustic needs of any city bumpkin or the most established gentleman farmer. No matter what you're looking for, from brass beds to buckets, wicker to weather vanes, rockers to real estate or curtains to crockery, you'll find them listed here in this comprehensive, yet selective series of categorical country listings.

Acreage

The "1980 National Roster of Realtors" lists an expansive membership of real estate agents and their branches in excess of 760,000! It is

easy then to imagine the thousands of realtors specializing in land, farms and country homes. The potential buyer, however, has two immediate and highly reliable sources which may be used to cut through this 1400-page encyclopedia of acreage and find exactly what he wants. First, Strout Realty has, by request, published a seasonal catalogue listing over 5000 country properties, described *and* pictured. Their offices total 700 and are located in some 43 states.

Then there's the United Farm Agency, which also puts out a catalogue listing some 300 farms, ranches, acreages and country homes. Their branches also stretch from coast to coast, and all you have to do is drop them a line and they'll drop their pamphlet in the mail.

STROUT REALTY INC.
60 East 42nd Street
Dept. 5390
New York, NY
10017

UNITED FARM AGENCY INC.
612-V West 47th Street
Kansas City, MO
64112
Call Toll Free 1-800-892-5785

Authentic Homes

Today, more than ever, new and prospective homeowners are discovering the joys and rewarding hard work that is part of owning a period house. Whether you already have a potential renovator's dream, would like to find one or would even like to have one built to historic precision, the following people and/or firms can help you. Here is a list of architects, restoration experts and consultants who are all trained and experienced in the field of making an old house look like "new" ... that is, the way it was 100 or more years ago.

If your tastes are more rustic, there is also a listing of major log home industries and companies, most of which have informative brochures available on request. Before you shrink in horror at the prospect of being "too primitive," take a look at some of the surprises these people have in store.

THE ACQUISITION &
   RESTORATION CORP.
1226 Broadway
Indianapolis, IA 46202
(317) 632-1461
(General contractors and
   designers)

ANNE W. BAKER RESTORATIONS
   INC.
670 Drift Road
Westport, MA 02790
(617) 636-8765
(General contracting and
   consultation)

BABCOCK BARN HOMES
P.O. Box 484
Williamstown, ME 01267
(413) 458-3334
(Barn to home creations)

DAVID HOWARD INC.
P.O. Box 295
Alstead, NH 03602
(603) 835-6356
(Across the miles dismantling and
   reassembly)

ELLEN BEASLEY
P.O. Box 1145
Galveston, TX 77553
(713) 762-9852
(Consultant)

HISTORIC BOULEVARD SERVICE
1520 West Jackson Blvd.
Chicago, IL 60607
(312) 829-6562
(Renovation and construction)

HOWELL CONSTRUCTION
2700 12th Avenue South
Nashville, TN 37204
(605) 269-5659
(Custom Homebuilders)

J. GORDON TURNBALL A.I.A.
Architecture/Preservation/
   Planning
15 Vandewater Street
San Francisco, CA 94133
(415) 788-3954
(Supervising Architects)

AIR LOCK LOG COMPANY INC.
P.O. Box 2506
Las Vegas, NM 87701

AUTHENTIC HOMES CORP.
P.O. Box 1288
Laramie, WY 82070

BOYNE FALLS LOG HOMES
Boyne Falls, MI 49713

LOK-N-LOGS, INC.
RR #2 Box 212
Sherbourne, NY 13460

NEW ENGLAND LOG HOMES INC.
P.O. Box 50506
Handen, CT 06518

NORTHEASTERN LOG HOMES
Box 7966-G
Louisville, KY 40207

THE RUSTICS OF LINDBERGH
LAKE INC.
Seeley Lake, MT 59808

WARD CABIN CO.
Box 72 Dept. CL
Houlton, ME 04730

WILDERNESS LOG HOMES
RR #2 GHCL 89
Plymouth, WI 53073

YELLOWSTONE LOG HOMES
RR #4 Box 2CJ
Rigby, ID 83442

Ashes to Ashes

Pot belly and wood-burning cook-stoves are very much alive and well in this new energy- and inflation-conscious society. Many companies are turning out authentically designed, attractive-looking heat sources for almost any room in the house. All dealers listed will provide you with picture and information booklets.

APACHE STOVE
Heritage Stove Mftg. Co.
P.O. Box 371
Marshville, NC 28103
(704) 624-2948

THE ASHLEY HEATER CO.
P.O. Box 128
Florence, AL 35630

THE ATLANTA STOVE WORKS
P.O. Box 5254
Atlanta, GA 30307

AURORA WOOD BURNING
  STOVES
Diversified Products Inc.
11300 Jefferson Avenue
Cincinnati, OH 45241

BETTER N' BEN'S WOODSTOVES
P.O. Box 526
150 New Britain Avenue
Unionville, CT 06085
(203) 673-2556

BICENTENNIAL STOVES
972 North Industrial Park Drive
Orem, UT 84057
(801) 226-0055

BIRMINGHAM STOVE AND RANGE
  CO.
P.O. Box 2647
Birmingham, AL 35202

BLUERIDGE MOUNTAIN STOVE
  WORKS
305 5th Avenue East
Hendersonville, NC 28739
(704) 697-2431

BRASILIAN STOVE WORKS
463-7 10th Avenue
New York, NY 10018
(212) 947-0690

BUFFALO STOVES INC.
812 East Ferry Street
Buffalo, NY 14211
(716) 896-4383

CAMDEN COOKSTOVE CO.
38 Union Street
Camden, ME 04834
(207) 236-2006

THE CAWLEY STOVE CO. INC.
27 North Washington Street
Boyertown, PA 19512
(215) 367-2643

CLASSIC STOVE WORKS
233 Main Street, Suite 608
New Britain, CT 06051
(203) 229-4772

COMFORTER STOVE WORKS
Box 175
Lochmere, NH 03252
(603) 528-1885

CRANE STOVE WORKS INC.
Box 440
Braintree, MA 02184

DON'S FIREPLACE FURNACE CO.
24430 South Highway, 99-E
Canby, OR 97013
(503) 266-2026

THE EARTH STOVE INC.
10425 SW Tualatin/Sherwood Rd.

Tualatin, OR 97062
(503) 648-5302

EMERALD WOOD BURNING
  STOVES
Carolina Fabrication of Traveler's
Rest Inc.
P.O. Box 664
Traveler's Rest, SC 29690
(803) 836-8124

ENERGY HARVESTERS CORP.
Route 12 Box 19
Fitzwilliam, NH 03347
(603) 585-3300

FIREKING STOVES OF UTAH INC.
Fireking International Inc.
205 Walker Bank Building
P.O. Box 10
Logan, UT 84321

FISHER STOVES INTERNATIONAL
  INC.
P.O. Box 10605
Eugene, OR 97440

FREEDOM STOVE WORKS
2700 Maple
Walled Lake, MI 48088
(313) 669-3737

GLACIER BAY INC.
14920 NE 95th Street
Redmond, WA 98052
(206) 881-5200

GODIN
Cohen and Peck Importers
14 Arrow Street
Cambridge, MA 02138
(617) 354-1459

GRANDFATHER STOVE
   MANUFACTURING CO.
P.O. Box 763 Hawkins Road
Traveler's Rest, SC 29690
(800) 845-4141

GRIZZLY STOVE WORKS
Derco, Inc., 10005 E. U.S. 233
Blissfield, MI 49228

HEARTHSTONE
RFD #1
Morrisville, VT 05661
(802) 888-4586

HOUSE OF WEBSTER
Box DE 181
Rogers, AR 72756

HURRICANE WOODSTOVES INC.
P.O. Box 327
Blackfoot, ID 83321
(208) 785-2121

KRISTIA ASSOCIATES
343 First Avenue P.O. Box 1118
Portland, ME 04104
(207) 772-2821

LAKEWOOD SOUTH INC.
Front and Prairie Streets
Conway, AR 72032
(501) 329-2957

LANGE WOODSTOVES
SVENDBORG Company Inc.
Bridgeman Block, P.O. Box 5
Hanover, NH 03775

MONARCH RANGES AND
   HEATERS
Beaver Dam, WI 53916
(414) 887-8131

NASHUA WOOD AND COAL
   STOVES
Heathdale Associates Inc.
Box 1039
Meredith, NH 03252
(603) 279-8118

OL' HICKORY WOODSTOVES
Box 8008
Greenville, SC 29602
(803) 277-2870

OLD TIMER MIDWEST STOVES
Mt. Vernin, IL 62864

ORLEY'S CUSTOM STOVES INC.
1370 Murfreesboro Road
Nashville, TN 37217

PENN STOVE
Mifflin County Industrial Plaza
Lewistown, PA 17044
(717) 242-1460

QUAKER STOVE CO., INC.
200 West Fifth Street
Landsdale, PA 19446
(215) 362-2019

RUSSO MANUFACTURING CORP.
87 Warren Street
Randolph, MA 02368
(617) 963-1182

SHRADER WOOD STOVES
600 South Seneca Road
Eugene, OR 97402
(503) 484-7331

SOLAR KEY WOOD STOVES
P.O. Box 575
Stayton, OR 97383
(503) 769-7761

THELIN-THOMPSON
P.O. Box 459
Kings Beach, CA 95719
(916) 546-4852

THER KON
207 East Mill Road
Galesville, WI 54630
(608) 582-2276

UNION MANUFACTURING CORP.
Boyertown, PA 19512
(215) 367-5360

WASHINGTON STOVE WORKS
P.O. Box 687
Everett, WA 98201
(206) 252-2148

WEBSTER STOVE FOUNDRY
125 West Lockwood
Webster Groves, MO 63119
(314) 962-0150

WOODLAND STOVES OF
   AMERICA INC.
1460 West Airline Highway
Waterloo, IA 50704
(319) 234-5567

WOODMASTER STOVES
Subran Manufacturing Company
Box 399
Dayton, TN 37321

WOOD STOVES
Bryant Steel Works
Thorndike, ME 04986
(207) 568-3663

If you have wooded acreage, it can be doubly profitable and environmentally sound to have a reputable logger come in and harvest your property. According to Dan Morgan, an independent logger in New York State, "Loggers aren't very popular. Nobody trusts us. They think we'll just strip the land." Not so. Overgrown trees and very thick groves ultimately spoil both forest and timber. But if logged properly, not only will the land owner walk away with a handsome bundle of cash from his timber, but he will have enough timber waste and excess branches to keep him in a supply of firewood for years! And even more important, the land can be harvested again in another 15 years. The second time around, it will yield an even better crop of timber and set up a self-perpetuating forest ... as well as a self-perpetuating income. And speaking of income, if you're planning on the welfare of future grandchildren, forget about the stock market! The word is BLACK WALNUT. They bring in BIG bucks for timber. *One tree,* aged approximately 50 years, was recently sold for a sum of $11,000 in timber. A forest of those could even make J. R. Ewing's mouth water!

If you're really into wood-burning stoves, cookstoves and wood/energy conservation, note the publication of a monthly magazine. It's called "Wood N' Energy"

176

and subscriptions are available. If you're interested you may write directly to them for more information.

WOOD N' ENERGY
P.O. Box 2008
Concord, NH 03301

Antiques, Auctions and Flea Markets

This section provides three valuable, nationwide listings for furnishing your country home with authentic pieces of furniture and country collectibles. Store hours, days and times of events and even locations may vary or change at the last minute, so it is advisable to call ahead first and make proper arrangements. The

dealers and markets listed are generally open weekends, year round, and specialize in antique furniture and various pieces of Americana. Although auctions and flea markets can be an inexpensive and surprising source of genuine articles, don't forget to check your own cellar or attic first.

ALABAMA

Chandler and Cooper Antiques
114 Gin Street
Springville, AL 35146
(205) 467-6371

Flomation Antique Auction
Herbert P. Heller, Auctioneer
Route 1, Box 196-A, 207 Palafox
   Street
Flomaton, AL 36441
(205) 296-3710

Gardendale Antique Mall
2455 Decatur
Gardendale, AL 35071
(205) 631-8869
(Tues.–Sun. 9–5)

ARIZONA

Bishop Gallery
7164 Main Street
Scottsdale, AZ 85251
(602) 949-9062

Antiques America
123 South Eastbourne,
#16 Broadway Village
Tuscon, AZ 85716
(602) 327-8697

Ledbetter's Auction Gallery
915 North Central Avenue
Phoenix, AZ 85004
(602) 257-1455

ARKANSAS

International Antiques, Inc.
4005 Landski Drive
North Little Rock, AR 72118
(501) 758-5167

Old Theatre Flea Market
116 South Second Street
Rogers, AR 72756
(501) 636-9824
(Mon.–Sat. 9–5)

CALIFORNIA

The Snow Goose Antiques
1010 Torrey Pines Road
La Jolla, CA 92037
(714) 454-4893

The Three Witches Antiques
2843 California Street
San Francisco, CA 94115
(415) 922-0940

Tin Duck Antiques
1329 West Washington Blvd.
Venice, CA 90291
(213) 396-3644

Chico Auction Gallery
Jack Harbour, Auctioneer
926 West Eighth Street
Chico, CA 95926
(916) 345-0431

Fresno Auction Service
Rex Irwin, Auctioneer

1516 H. Street
Fresno, CA 93721
(209) 486-8402

Baker's Auction
Dean Baker, Auctioneer
14100 Paramount Boulevard
Paramount, CA 90723
(213) 531-1524

Rose Bowl Antique Flea Market
Rose Bowl at Brookside Park
Pasadena, CA
R. G. Canning Enterprises
P.O. Box 400, Maywood 90270
(213) 587-5100
(2nd Sun. of every month)

Auction City and Flea Market
8521 Folsom Boulevard
Sacramento, CA 95826
(916) 383-0950
(Sat.–Sun. 9–5)

COLORADO

Bishop Gallery
South Vrain Highway
Allenspark, CO 80510
(303) 747-2419

Connell Auctions
Bob Connell, Auctioneer
200 First St., P.O. Box 1027
Ault, CO 80610
(303) 834-1113

Mile High Flea Market, Inc.
5200 East Sixty-fourth Ave.
Commerce City, CO 80022
(303) 289-4656
(Sat.–Sun. 6–5)

CONNECTICUT

Falcon Antiques
184 Main Street
Old Wethersfield, CT 06109
(203) 529-7262

J. B. Richardson Gallery
362 Pequot Avenue
Southport, CT 06490
(203) 259-1903

Ravenwood Antiques
Rte. L, Box 297, Hickory Lane
Bethlehem, CT 06751
(203) 266-7050

Country Auction Gallery
Steven Smith, Auctioneer
1140 Main Street (Route 31)
Coventry, CT 06238
(203) 742-9698

Villa's Auction Gallery
Richard Villa, Auctioneer
Route 44
Norfolk, CT 06058
(203) 542-5626

The Elephant's Trunk Bazaar
Route 7
New Milford, CT 06810
(203) 355-1448
(Sun., May–Oct.)

Tique Mart
Route 6
Woodbury, CT 06762
R. H. Sprano Middlebury Rd.
Middlebury, CT 06762
(203) 758-1571
(Sat., Late April–Nov.)

DELAWARE

The Hudson House
Benson St. and Route 1
Rehoboth Beach, DE 19971
(302) 227-2487

Paris N. Walters
Box 365
Newark, DE 19711
(302) 737-5883

Wilson's Auction Sales
Dave Wilson, Auctioneer
Route 113, P.O. Box 84
Lincoln, DE 19960
(302) 422-3454

Sebul's Antiques & Galleries
775 South DuPont Highway
New Castle, DE 19720
(302) 834-0500
(Sat., Sun., Mon.)

DISTRICT OF COLUMBIA

Cherishables
1816 Jefferson Place N.W.
D.C. 20036
(202) 785-4087

Georgetown Flea Market
Wisconsin Avenue and S St.
D.C. 20036
Contact: Michael Vezo
(202) 333-0289
(Sun. March–Nov. 9–6)

FLORIDA

Brian Riba
112 Court South
West Palm Beach, FL 33405
(305) 832-6737

Maze Pottinger
1160 North Federal Highway
Ft. Lauderdale, FL 33304
(305) 463-4518

Rose Plummer Ltd., Antiques
2909 E. Commercial Blvd.
Ft. Lauderdale, FL 33308
(305) 491-4060

Foxhall Antique Gallery
Dan Sexton, Auctioneer
8500 Cortez Road
Bradenton, FL 33505
(813) 792-7508

Allandale Flea Market
5008 Ridgewood Avenue
Daytona Beach, FL 92019
(904) 767-7229
(Sat.–Sun. 7–5)

The Flea Market
1370 Capitol Circle NW
Tallahassee, FL 32304
(904) 576-4950
(Sat.–Sun. 11–6)

GEORGIA

Deanne Levison
American Antiques
1935 Peachtree Rd. NE
Atlanta, GA 30309
(404) 355-0106

Pardue's Antique Auctions
Claud Pardue, Auctioneer
Route 1
Talmo, GA 30575
(404) 693-2500

Delight's Antique and Flea Market

Pete DeSantis, Jr., Auctioneer
Pavo Road
Thomasville, GA 31792
(912) 226-8849

Elce's Georgia Antique and Flea
  Market
Lakewood Fairgrounds
Atlanta, GA 30308
(404) 872-1913
(2nd wknd, every month, Sat.
  9–6, Sun. 10–6)

ILLINOIS

Apple Barn Antiques
2526 Rock Springs Road
Decatur, IL 62500
(217) 422-1784

House of Seven Fables
300 East Dale Street
Somonauk, IL 60552
(815) 498-2289

Puffabelly Station
Route 136 (I-55)
McLean, IL 61754
(309) 874-2112

The Trading Post
401 North East Street
Olney, IL 62450
(618) 498-2289

Antique Exchange Auctions
Mike Jeremiah, Auctioneer
417 East Broadway
Alton, IL 62002
(618) 462-4881

Greater Rockford Antiques and
   Flea Market
Highway 51 and Sandy Hollow Rd.
Rockford, IL
Contact: Jerry Shorkey
6350 Canyon Wood
Rockford, IL 61109
(815) 397-6687
(Sat.–Sun. 8–5)

INDIANA

Dovetail Antiques
101 Dewey Avenue
Washington, IN 47501
(812) 254-7622

The Mare's Nest
US 40 West, Route 1, Box 549
Cambridge, IN 47327
(317) 478-5941

Red Barn Antiques
325 East 106 Street
Indianapolis, IN 46280
(317) 846-8929

Doug Davies
Doug Davies, Auctioneer
Delphi Armory
Highway 18
Delphi, IN 46923
(317) 563-3600

Antique Flea Market
Indiana State Fairgrounds
Agriculture Building
Indianapolis, IN 46201
(317) 674-6450
(Sat. 10–7, Sun. 10–5)

Big Red Flea Market
11777 Lafayette Rd.

P.O. Box 415
Zionsville, IN 46077
(317) 769-3266
(Fri.–Sun.)

IOWA

Renaissance
Mike Hammes, Auctioneer
Box 4
Guernsey, IA 50172
(319) 685-4251

Bryant Auction Service
Richard Bryant, Auctioneer
R. 3, Box 245
Keokuk, IA 52632
(319) 463-7727

Central Iowa Fair Flea Market
Fairgrounds, Route 2
Marshaltown, IA 50158
(515) 753-3671
(For day and place: contact
   Carole Storjohann (515) 474-
   2452)

KANSAS

Woody Auction and Real Estate
   Co.
John M. Woody, Auctioneer
212 East Fourth, P.O. Box 618
Douglass, KS 67039
(316) 746-2694

Quantril's Flea Market
811 New Hampshire Street
Lawrence, KS 66044
Contact: Randolph S. Davis
(913) 841-1325
(Sat.–Sun. 10–5)

KENTUCKY

Finders Keepers Antiques
115 East Main Street
Flemingsburg, KY 41041
(606) 759-7738

Sapp Brothers Antiques
East Broadway/Highway 208
Campbellsville, KY 42718
(502) 789-1497

Woodford Landing Antiques
185 South Main
Versailles, KY 40383
(606) 876-6505

E'Town Flea Market
Highway 31W North
Elizabethtown, KY 42701
(502) 737-6361
Contact: Bill Koutt
Route 8 Box 120, Elizabethtown
(Fri.–Sun.)

LOUISIANA

Sanchez Antiques and Auction
   Galleries
T. Sanchez, Auctioneer
4730 Magazine Street
New Orleans, LA 70115
(504) 524-0281

Ponchatoula Auction Company
Harry Hunt, Auctioneer
Main Street
Ponchatoula, LA 70454
(504) 386-8974

190 Trading Post Flea Market
Route 2, Box 445 A
Lacombe, LA 70445
(504) 882-5336
(Sat.–Sun. 10–5)

MAINE

Bell and Kettle Antiques
Routes 113 and 5
East Brownfield, ME 04010
(207) 935-3182

Cranberry Hill Antiques
Route 1
Cape Neddick, ME 03902
(207) 363-5178

Maple Avenue Antiques
23 Maple Avenue
Farmington, ME 04938
(207) 778-4850

Pumpkin Patch
Route 1
Searsport, ME 04974
(207) 548-6047

Mayo Auctioneers and Appraisers,
  Inc.
Leonard Mayo, Auctioneer
RFD 1, Box 285
Ellsworth, ME 04605
(207) 667-8062

Julia's Auction Service
James D. Julia, Auctioneer
Route 201
Fairfield, ME 04937
(207) 453-9725

Bo-Mar Hall Flea Market and
  Antique Gallery
Route 1, P.O. Box 308
Wells, ME 04090
(207) 646-8843
(Daily 9–5)

MARYLAND

Comus Antiques
North Federal Street
New Market, MD 21774
(301) 831-6464

Jerry E. Tiller
Route 1, Box 55
Pocomoke, MD 21851
(301) 957-0429

The Willow Tree
11905 Devilwood Drive
Potomac, MD 20854
(301) 762-3748

American Auction Gallery
C.P. Jacobs, Jr., Auctioneer
Route 70 East
Frederick, MD 21701
(301) 662-3530

Town and Country Auctions
Houck Avenue
Hampstead, MD 21074
(301) 239-7776

Farmers Market Flea Market
9919 Pulaski Highway (Hwy 40)
Baltimore, MD 21220
(301) 687-5505
(Sat.–Sun., Apr.–Nov., 7–5)

Rhodside Flea Market
Route 15 and Biggs Ford Rd.
Frederick, MD 21701
(301) 898-7502
(Fri.–Sun., Apr.–Nov.)

MASSACHUSETTS

Chesire Village Antiques
Route 8

Chesire, MA 01225
(413) 743-4385

Jos. Kilbridge
Antiques of Early America
Main Street (Route 119)
Groton, MA 01450
(617) 448-3330

Penelope W. Princi
Penelope's Primitives
P.O. Box 8
Hyannis Port, MA 02647
(617) 775-8844

Tranquil Corners Antiques
38 Center Street
Nantucket, MA 02554
(617) 228-0848

Robert W. Skinner, Inc.
Robert W. Skinner, Jr., Auctioneer
Route 117
Bolton, MA 01740
(617) 779-5528
585 Boylston Street
Boston MA 02116
(617) 236-1700

Louis E. Caropreso Auctions
P.O. Box 1791
Lenox, MA 01240
(413) 243-2446

Antiques Flea Market
Cordage Park
Plymouth, MA 02360
(617) 837-6665
Contact: Paul Reynolds (617) 834-
  6709
(Sun.)

Antique Marketplace
Shetland Industrial Park
29 Congress Street
Salem, MA 01970
(617) 745-9393
(Sun. 9–5)

MICHIGAN

Amariah Antiques
Amariah Prouty House
302 Elm Street
Kalamazoo, MI 49007
(616) 345-4474

Tim and Pam Hill
56000 Ten Mile Road
South Lyon, MI 48178
(313) 437-1538

Stalker and Boos, Inc.
David Stalker and Frank Boos III,
   Auctioneers
280 North Woodward
Birmingham, MI 48011
(313) 646-4560

New Gian Flea Market
5350 Davison Road
Burton-Flint, MI 48509
(313) 742-5371
Contact: Jerry Keely
(313) 639-2810
(Fri. 12–9, Sat.–Sun. 9–6)

MINNESOTA

Robert J. Riesberg
1349 Delaware Avenue
Saint Paul, MN 55118
(612) 457-1772

Central Auction Co.
Charles W. Weinberger,
   Auctioneer
4020 Central Avenue
Minneapolis, MN 55421
(612) 781-0300

Rainbow Bait Flea Market
Box 302, Highway 78N
Battle Lake, MN 56515
(218) 864-5569
Contact: Lori Edlund
(218) 864-5513
(Sat.–Sun., May–Sept.)

MISSISSIPPI

7 C's Antiques
103 North Lamar Street
Oxford, MS 38655
(601) 234-2088

C.S.A. Auction Company
Conny Dixon, Auctioneer
1805 Highway 15 North
Ripley, MS 38663
(601) 837-8148

Trading Post
101 Porter Avenue
Ocean Springs, MS 39564
Contact: Pat Bills
(601) 875-2981

MISSOURI

The Auction Barn
Bud Jones, Auctioneer
3418 West Division
Springfield, MO 65804
(417) 831-2734

Joplin Flea Market

1200 Block Virginia Avenue
Joplin, MO 64801
Contact: Ed Frazier
(417) 623-6328
(Sat.–Sun. 8–5)

Olde Town Antique Mall and Flea
   Market
600 Booneville
Springfield, MO 65806
Contact: Thelma Wright
(417) 831-6665

NEW HAMPSHIRE

Burlwood Antique Shop
Route 3
Meredith, NH 03253
(603) 279-6387

Brick House Antiques
McKinley Circle
Marlborough, NH 03455
(603) 876-7765

October Stone Antiques
Jady Hill
Exeter, NH 03833
(603) 772-2024

The Rooster Antiques
RFD #4
Concord, NH 03301
(603) 798-5912

Brookline Auction Gallery
Ronald and William Pelletier,
   Auctioneers
Proctor Hill Road (Rte 130)
Brookline, NH 03033
(603) 673-4474

Paul McInnis, Inc.
Paul McInnis, Auctioneer
Route 1, Box 97
Hampton Falls, NH 03844
(603) 926-3982

Outdoor Antique Market
Route 122
Amherst, NH 03031
Contact: Carlson Mgmt.
(617) 641-0600
(Sun. mid-Apr.–Nov. 6–3)

Grand View Farm Antique and
 Flea Market
Junction of Route 28 and 28 By-
 Pass
Derry, NH 03038
Contact: Albert Gidley
(603) 432-2326

NEW JERSEY

Bogwater Jim Antiques
Route 15
Lafayette, NJ 07848
(201) 383-8170

Cedar House Antiques
Oceanview Drive
Toms River, NJ 08753
(201) 929-0573

Governor's Antique Market
Route 179 North
Lambertville, NJ 08530
(609) 397-2010
(Sat.–Sun. 8–5)

NEW MEXICO

Habitat
222 Shelby

Santa Fe, NM 87501
(505) 982-3722

Pattin Auction Company
Ronald Pattin, Auctioneer
411 Marble Northeast
Albuquerque, NM 87102
AUCTIONS: 6403 Coor Southwest
Albuquerque 87105
(505) 242-6329

NEW YORK

The Black Barn Antiques
P.O. Box 1080
Montauk Highway
Bridgehampton, NY 11932
(516) 324-2112

Greenwillow Farm Ltd.
Raup Road
Chatham, NY 12037
(518) 392-9654

Ths. K. Woodard
American Antiques & Quilts
1022 Lexington Avenue
New York, NY 10021
(212) 988-2906

Union Valley Antiques
RD #1, Box 133
Bainbridge, NY 13733
(607) 967-8262

Bill Rinaldi Auctions
Bill Rinaldi, Mike Fallon,
 Auctioneers
Box 85
Pleasant Valley, NY 12569
AUCTIONS: Bedell Road
Poughkeepsie, NY

(914) 454-9613

Iroquois Auctions
Gerald A. Petro, Auctioneer
Broad Street
Port Henry, NY 12974
(518) 942-3355

Tarrytown Flea Market
635 South Broadway
Tarrytown, NY 10591
Contact: Russell Carrell, Salisbury,
 CT
(203) 435-9301

NORTH CAROLINA

Briar Patch Antiques
2185 Knight Road
Kernersville, NC 27284
(919) 993-8254

Ellington's Antiques
3050 Medlin Drive
Raleigh, NC 27607
(919) 781-2383

Griffin's Antiques
Route 7, Box 958
Greensboro, NC 27407
(919) 454-3362

Childs Auction Company, Inc.
P.O. Drawer 1
Sanford, NC 27330
(919) 775-7618

Pfafftown Jaycee Antique Flea
  Market
West Central Community Center
Yadkinville Road
Pfafftown, NC 27040
(919) 945-5687
Contact: Bob Lohmeyer
(919) 765-8291

OHIO

The Brass Bell Antiques
331 North High Street
Chillicothe, OH 45601
(614) 773-1500

Country Wagon Antiques
427 North Street
Chardon, OH 44024
(216) 286-3842

The Iron Kettle
129 North Wolf Creek Street
Brookville, OH 45309
(513) 833-2526

Ohio Country Furniture
2609 Stratford Road
Delaware, OH 43015
(614) 363-1027

Early Auction Company
Roger Early and Son, Auctioneers
123 Main Street
Milford, OH 45150
(513) 831-4855

Belle Fontaine Flea Market
Logan County Fairground
Belle Fontaine, OH 43311
(513) 592-1626
(Sat.–Sun. 9–5)

Farm and Flea Market
1270 Route 22 West
Washington Court House
OH 43160
(614) 335-8780
(Sat.–Sun, 9–6)

OKLAHOMA

Lawton Flea Market Inc.
1130 East Gore Boulevard
Lawton, OK 73501
Joseph Reynolds
(405) 355-1292
(Fri.–Sun., 1st and 3rd wknd of
  each month)

Persimmon Hollow Antique
Village and Flea Market
Seventy-first St. and Garnett Road
Tulsa, OK 74107
(918) 252-7113
(Sat.–Sun. 9–5)

OREGON

Springers Flea Market
18300 SE Richey Road
Portland, OR 97236
(503) 665-3568
(Sat.–Sun. 9:30–5)

Sunday Flea Market
Memorial Coliseum
Portland, OR 97212
(503) 246-9996
(Sundays)

PENNSYLVANIA

Ironmasters Mansion Antiques
Route 29
Green Lane, PA 18054
(215) 234-8863

Olde Hope Antiques
Box 69C, Route 202
New Hope, PA 18938
(215) 794-8161

Willowdale Antiques
101 East Street Road
Kennett Square, PA 19348
(215) 444-5377

Yellow Barn Antiques
Box 145
Center Valley, PA 18034
(215) 282-4965

Clements and Sons
Joe Clements, Auctioneer
11 South Lansdowne Avenue
Lansdowne, PA 19050
(215) 622-9825

Renninger's Antique Market
Route 22
Denver, PA 17517
(215) 267-2177
(Sun. 7–5)

RHODE ISLAND

The Farmers Daughter
Route 2, South County Trail
Exeter, RI 02822
(401) 295-8493

Hickory Hollow Antiques
Trimtown Road
North Scituate, RI 02857
(401) 647-5321

Jack Martone, Auctioneer
290 Pulaski Street
Coventry, RI 02816
(401) 826-1564

Americana Flea Market
Rocky Hill Fairgrounds
East Greenwich, RI 62852
(401) 884-6020
(Sun. Apr. 15–Dec. 15 5–5)

SOUTH CAROLINA

Coles and Company Inc.
84 Wentworth Street
Charleston, SC 29401
(803) 723-2142

Garden Gate Antiques
96 King Street
Charleston, SC 29401
(803) 722-0308

The Cattle Barn Flea Market
912 Poinsett Highway
Greenville, SC 29608
(803) 242-3092
(Wed and Fri. 12–9, Sat. 7–9, Sun.
  1–6)

TENNESSEE

Evelyn Anderson Galleries
Westgate Center Highway 100
Nashville, TN 37205
(615) 352-6770

Trace Tavern Antiques
Malvern and Delle Brown
8456 Highway 100
Nashville, TN 37221
(615) 646-5600

Estate Gallery
Larry Sims, Auctioneer
115 West Vine Street
P.O. Box 87
Murfreesboro, TN 37130
(615) 890-2067

Parkland Flea Market
Route 6
Lebanon, TN 37087
(615) 444-9915
(Sat.–Sun. 7 til dark)

TEXAS

Clements Antiques of Texas Inc.
P.O. Box 727
Forney, TX 75126
(214) 226-1520

Robert Kinnerman and Brian
  Ramaekers
River Oaks Center at
2002 Peden Street
Houston, TX 77019
(713) 526-0095

A-1 Auction House
Ross Lucas, Auctioneer
1905 South Shaver
Pasadena, TX 77502
(713) 472-3777

County Weekend Common Market
5115 South Shaver
Houston, TX 77034
(713) 947-8522
(Sat.–Sun. 7–7)

VERMONT

Ethan Allen Antiques Shop Inc.
1626 Williston Road
South Burlington, VT 65401
(802) 863-3764

Ice Pond Farm Antiques
Box 2753
East Arlington, VT 05252
(802) 375-6448

Sign of the Raven
Main Street
Saxton's River, VT 05154
(802) 869-2500

Manchester Flea Market
Route 11 and 30
Manchester Center, VT 05255
(802) 362-1631
(Sat., May–Oct.)

VIRGINIA

Cochrans Antiques
P.O. Box 74
Purcellville, VA 22132
(703) 338-7395

Dor Mil Antiques
P.O. Box 693, Courthouse Station
Arlington, VA 22216
(703) 243-8455

Worcester House Antiques
US 13
New Church, VA 23415
(804) 824-3847

Wilson Galleries
Dean and Mark Wilson,
  Auctioneers
P.O. Box 102
Fort Defiance, VA 24437

Verona Antique Market and Wharf
  Antique Mall
P.O. Box 317
Verona, VA 24482
(703) 885-0485
(Thur.–Fri. 10–5)

WASHINGTON

Sea-Tac Flea Market
34300 Pacific Highway South
Federal Way, WA 98003
(206) 838-0797
(Sat.–Sun. 10–6)

Angle Lake Flea Market
19832 Pacific Highway South
Seattle, WA 98182
(206) 878-8161
Contact: John Brewer
(206) 255-2039
(Thur.–Sun. 10–6)

WEST VIRGINIA

Seeley Pine Furniture and
    Antiques
Route 522 South
Berkley Springs, WV 25411

Sun Valley Flea
Pipe Stem Drive-In Theatre
Athens Hinton State Route
Athens, WV 24712
(304) 384-7382
(Sat.–Sun.)

WISCONSIN

Jaeger Antiques
459 South Randall Avenue
Janesville, WI 53545
(608) 754-8585

Milwaukee Auction Galleries
Gary Hollander, Auctioneer
4747 West Bradley Road
Milwaukee, WI 53223
(414) 355-5054

Summer Flea Market

Shawano County Fairgrounds
Highway 29
Shawano, WI 54166
(715) 526-9285
Contact: Bob Zurko
(715) 526-9472

WYOMING

Art's Auction House
Arthur Mahnke, Auctioneer
216 South Main
Lusk, WY 82225
(307) 334-3779

For the serious collector, there
are several magazines, most of
them monthly, which include interesting articles, photographic
essays, auction news, show dates,
classified departments and much,
much more. Several of them are
listed below.

Antique Monthly
P.O. Drawer 2
Tuscaloosa, AL 35402

The Antique Trader Weekly
P.O. Box 1050
Dubuque, IA 52001

The Magazine ANTIQUES
551 Fifth Avenue
New York, NY 10017

Maine Antique Digest
Jefferson Street
Box 358
Waldoboro, ME 04572

Ohio Antique Review

P.O. Box 538
Worthington, OH 43085

Spinning Wheel
Antiques and Early Crafts
American Antiques and Crafts
    Society
Fame Avenue
Hanover, PA 17331

Accents and Accessories

A braided rug for that space by
the hearth, a copper rooster
weather vane, some ornate handles for the pine cabinets and
some spatterware; a shaker wash-
stand and a quilt for the bedroom
and yes, even a wooden bathtub
for the bath. "Accents and Accessories" lists manufacturers and
craftsmen who specialize in fine
pieces of American art and reproduction pieces that will give that
touch of authenticity to country-
style life. Several of the sources
from each section do not sell di-

rectly to the public, but will supply you with a listing of their distributors. Some have colorful catalogues as well as mail service.

CURTAINS, QUILTS, AND COUNTRY LINENS

Colonial Maid Curtains
Depot Plaza
Marmaroneck, NY 10543
(914) 698-6136
(Early American-style curtains)

Constance Carol
Box 899
Plymouth, MA 02360
(617) 746-6116
(Early American-style curtains
    many other store locations in
    MA, VA and PA)

Goodwin Weavers
Blowing Rock Crafts, Inc.
P.O. Box 314
Blowing Rock, NC 28605
(704) 295-3577
(Woven table linens)

Homespun Weavers
169 Ridge Street
Emmaus, PA 18049
(215) 967-4550
(Cotton table linens and towels)

Marjorie S. Yoder
North Street, Box 181
Morgantown, PA 19543
(215) 286-5490
(Hand-stenciled table and bed
    linens)

Quilts and Other Comforts

Box 394, 6700 West 44th Avenue
Wheat Ridge, CO 80033
(Quilt kits)

Shanti Benoit
Magic Corner Quilts
42255 Little Lake Road
Mendicino, CA 95460
(707) 937-0825
(Quilts)

Sunshine Lane
Box 262 East
Millersburg, OH 44654
(Amish design quilts)

FLOORS AND WALLS

Adams and Swett
380 Dorchester Avenue
Boston, MA 02127
(617) 268-8000
(Hand-braided wool rugs)

Adele Bishop, Inc.
P.O. Box 122
Dorset, VT 05251
(802) 867-2235
(Stencil kits and supplies for
    fabrics, walls, floors and
    furniture)

Betty Emerson
108 New Haven Road
Oak Ridge, TN 37830
(615) 482-2943
(Woven mats and rugs)

The Collector's Choice
404 East 14th St., Apt. 5
New York, NY 10009
(212) 254-7744
(Wool braided rugs)

Laura A. Copenhaver
"Rosemont"
P.O. Box 145
Marion, VA 24354
(703) 783-4663
(Hooked rugs)

Stenciled Interiors
Hinman Lane
Southbury, CT 06488
(203) 264-8000
(Custom floor and wall stenciling)

FURNITURE AND LIGHTING

Antiquity Handcrafted Artifacts
    Inc.
255 North Barron Street
Eaton, OH 45320
(513) 456-3388
(Early American-style lighting,
    lanterns, tinware, candlesticks
    and molds)

Bedlam Brass Beds
19–21 Fairlawn Avenue
Fairlawn, NJ 07410
(201) 796-7200

Bittersweet
P.O. Box 5
Riverton, VT 05668
(802) 485-8562
(Handcrafted primitive furniture,
    clocks, tables. Custom work.)

The Candle Cellar and Emporium
1914 North Main Street
Fall River, MA 02720
(617) 679-6057

Douglas Campbell Co.
31 Bridge Street
Newport, RI 02840
(401) 846-4711
(Extensive selection of antique
  furniture reproductions)

Emperor Clock Co.
Dept 770, Emperor Industrial Park
Fairhope, AL 36532
(Grandfather and Early American
  clocks)

The Ethan Allen Co.
Ethan Allen Drive
Danbury, CT 06810
(203) 743-8000
(Early American Furniture
  reproductions)

Guild of Shaker Crafts
401 W. Savidge
Spring Lake, MI 49456
(616) 846-2870
(Extensive Shaker furniture
  replicas)

Habersham Plantation
P.O. Box 1209
Toccoa, GA 30577
(404) 886-1476
(American primitive furniture)

Heritage Lanterns
70 A Main Street
Yarmouth, ME 04096
(207) 846-3911
(Reproductions of Early American
  lighting, lanterns, sconces and
  chandeliers.)

The Hitchcock Chair Co.

Riverton, CT 06065
(203) 379-8531
(Hand-stenciled traditional maple
  furniture)

The Lovechest Co.
P.O. Box P-99
South Darmouth, MA 02748
(Large selection of chests)

Newton Millham Star Forge
672 Drift Road
Westport, MA 02790
(617) 636-5437
(18th-century lighting, candle
  holders, table and floor
  candlestands)

Pinewood Primitives
Route 9, Box 97 Dept CH34
Benton, KY 42025
(Pine furniture)

R. W. Alexander
Yesterday's Yankee
Lakeville, CT 06039
(203) 435-9539
(Extensive selection of
  handcrafted American furniture
  plus antique restoration
  services)

The Rocker Shop of Marietta
  Georgia
1421 White Circle, N.W.
P.O. Box 12
Marietta, GA 30061
(404) 427-2618
(Rockers, chairs, porch swings)

Stanton Woodcraft
Airport Road, P.O. Box 516
Stanton, KY 40380

(606) 663-4246
(Handcrafted Appalachian
  furniture)

Thos. Moser, Cabinet Makers
Cobbs Bridge Road
New Gloucester, ME 04260
(207) 926-4446
(Custom, handmade chests,
  trundle beds, cupboards,
  harvest tables and more)

Virginia Metalcrafters Inc.
1010 East Main Street
Waynesboro, VA 22980
(703) 942-8205
(Fireplace accessories, door
  knockers and door stops)

POTTERY, PANS AND PEWTER

Ball Corp.
345 South High Street
Munsie, IN 47305
(317) 747-6100
(Mason jars for canning)

Beaumont Heritage Pottery
Beach Ridge Road, Box 293
York, ME 03909
(207) 363-5878
(Handcrafted pottery)

Linda and Andre Brousseau
The Elements Pottery
639 North 3rd Street
Danville, KY 40422
(606) 236-7467
(Stoneware and dinnerware)

Denby Ltd., Inc.
130 Campus Plaza
Edison, NJ 08817
(201) 225-4710
(Country-style stoneware)

The Robinson-Ransbottom Pottery
   Co.
Roseville, OH 43777
(614) 697-7355
(Blue and brown spatterware)

Rubel and Co.
225 Fifth Avenue
New York, NY 10010
(212) 683-4400
(Glassware, hand-painted tinware,
   pewter and brass)

HARDWARE AND TUB-WARE

Domestic Environmental
   Alternatives
495 Main St., P.O. Box 1020
Murphy's, CA 95247
(209) 728-3860
(Antique bathroom fixtures)

Fife's Woodworking and
   Manufacturing
Route 107
Northwood, NH 03261
(603) 942-8339
(Handcrafted wooden bathroom
   accessories)

D. James Barnett, Blacksmith
710 W. Main Street
Plano, IL 60545
(312) 552-3675
(Hooks, hangers, hinges and
   hardware)

John Graney
Bear Creek Forge
Route 2, Box 135
Spring Green, WI 53588
(608) 588-2032
(Colonial kitchen and fireplace
   hardware)

Victorian Reproduction
   Enterprises
1601 Park Avenue South
Minneapolis, MN 55404
(612) 338-3636
(Antique plumbing fixtures and
   hardware)

Wheaton Village
Millville, NJ 08332
(609) 825-6800 ext. 504
(Handcrafted tinware, glass and
   pottery)

The Yankee Peddler
Burkart Bros., Inc.
Verplanck, NY 10596
(914) 737-7900

WOOD, WEAVERS AND WEATHER
VANES

Coker Creek Crafts
P.O. Box 95
Coker Creek, TN 37314
(615) 261-2157
(Handmade white oak baskets)

The Decorator Emporium
   Hardware, Inc.
353 Main Street
Danbury, CT 06810
(203) 748-2648
(Handmade weather vanes)

D. Ritter
101 North Haggin

P.O. Box 2108
Red Lodge, MT 59068
(406) 446-1227
(Hand-carved waterfowl)

Fran's Basket House
Route 10
Succasunna, NJ 07876
(201) 584-2230
(Handcrafted wicker and rattan
   importers)

The Magnificent Doll
209 East 60th Street
New York, NY 10022
(212) 753-7425
(Early American Dolls)

Mainly Baskets
1771 Tully Circle, N.E.
Atlanta, GA 30329
(404) 634-7664
(Americana basket reproductions)

MaLeck Industries, Inc.
P.O. Box 247
Wingate, NC 28174
(704) 233-4032
(Soap and bath accessories)

Joe and Jayne Byrne Panzarella
High Point Crafts
RD 2, Sky High Road
Tully, NY 13159
(315) 696-8540
(Fireplace brooms, feather dusters
   and bellows)

Peterboro Basket Co.
Peterboro, NH 03458
(603) 924-3861
(Early American baskets and
   buckets)

Ship N' Out
934 Harmony Road
Pawling, NY 12564
(914) 878-4901
(Copper weather vanes)

West Ridge Baskets, Inc.
Box 24
Rindge, NH 03461
(603) 899-2231
(Handwoven New England
    baskets)

In addition to these specialty companies, there are country stores and general stores that specialize in anything and everything. They are a delight to visit and browse through, and many contain one-of-a-kind items, crafts and bargains. All the stores listed have mail-order services available, so if you can't stop in and visit for a spell, try some country shopping by mail.

Cumberland General Store
Route 3
Crossville, TN 38555
(615) 484-8481

The Gazebo
660 Madison Avenue
New York, NY 10021
(212) 832-7077

L. L. Bean, Inc.
Freeport, ME 04033
(207) 865-3111

Ozark Mountain Collection
7 Downing Street

P.O. Box 507
Hollister, MO 65672
(417) 334-5788

The Renovators Supply
71 Northfield Road
Miller's Falls, MA 01349
(413) 659-3542
The Silo
Hunt Hill Farm
Upland Road RFD #3
New Milford, CT 06776
(203) 355-0300

Southern Highland Handicraft
    Guild
P.O. Box 9545, 15 Reddick Rd.
Asheville, NC 28805
(704) 298-7928

Tibor and Gail General Store
Dept TG, 636 Wildwood Avenue
Salamanca, NY 14779

Arts and Crafts

There has been a sudden re-awakening of interest in American arts and crafts over the last decade. Craftsmasters and their shows and fairs are as numerous and sporadic as mushrooms in a cow pasture. There are an estimated 1400 *major* events in the United States every year. Since such a list could comprise a book of its own, the section here narrows itself to the addresses of State Arts Councils, State Craft Councils and several valuable

magazines for the craftsmaster, beginner or buyer. Write to your own individual council, or that of a state nearby, and request a list of the crafts events ahead.

Alabama State Council on the Arts
    and Humanities
M.J. Zakrewski
The Gallagher House
114 North Hull Street
Montgomery, AL 36130

State Arts Council
Mrs. Louise Tester
6330 N. 7th Street
Phoenix, AZ 85014

Craft Directory
Sharon Heidingsfelder
P.O. Box 391
Little Rock, AR 72203

State Arts Council
Ed Harrison
Grant Humphrey's Mansion
770 Penny Street
Denver, CO 80203

State Arts Council
Anthony Keller
340 Capital Avenue
Hartford, CT 06106

The Crafts Fair Guide
Lee Speigel/Editor/Publisher
152 Buena Vista
Mill Valley, CA 94941

State Arts Council
Don Shulman
State Office Building
820 N. French Street
Wilmington, DE 19801

State Arts Council
Rebecca Kushner
Division of Cultural Affairs
Dept. of State, The Capital
Tallahassee, FL 32304

Georgia Council Crafts Program
Anna Johannaber
1627 Peachtree Street
Suite 205
Atlanta, GA 30309
(Exceptional crafts program)

State Arts Council
Carl J. Petrick
Statehouse Mail
Boise, ID 83720

State Arts Council
Clark Mitze
111 N. Wabash Avenue #700
Chicago, IL 60602

Indiana Arts Commission
Nancy R. Mead
155 E. Market Street
Indianapolis, IN 46204

Kansas Arts Commission
Columbia Building
112 West 6th Street
Suite 401
Topeka, KS 66603

The Kentucky Arts Commission
Jane Julian
Frankfort, KY 40601

State Arts Council
Al Head
Division of Arts P.O. Box 44247
Baton Rouge, LA 70801

Directory
United Maine Craftsmen
P.O. Box 193
Belfast, ME 04915

State Arts Council
Kenneth Kahn
15 W. Mulberry
Baltimore, MD 21201

Society of Arts and Crafts
175 Newbury Street
Boston, MA 02108

State Arts Council
E. Ray Scott
1200 6th Avenue
Executive Plaza
Detroit, MI 48226

Arts Resource and Information
  Center
Minneapolis Institute of Art
2400 Third Avenue
Minneapolis, MN 55404

State Arts Council
Lida Rogers
301 N. Lamar Street
Jackson, MS 39205

State Arts Council
Mary De Hahn
706 Chestnut Street
St. Louis, MO 63101

State Arts Council
David E. Nelson
1280 South Third Street W
Missoula, MT 59801

State Arts Council
Robin Tryloff
8448 W. Center Road
Omaha, NE 68124

New Hampshire Commission on
  the Arts
Phenix Hall
40 North Main Street
Concord, NH 03301

State Arts Council
Eileen Lawton
109 W. State Street
Trenton, NJ 08608

State Arts Council
Bernard Blas Lopez
113 Lincoln
Santa Fe, NM 87503

State Arts Council
Theodore Striggles
80 Centre Street
New York, NY 10013

North Dakota Arts Council
Glenn Scott
309 Mainard Hall
North Dakota State University
Fargo, ND 58102

Ohio Arts and Crafts Guild
9 North Main Street
Mount Vernon, OH 43050

State Arts Council
Ben Di Salvo
Jim Thorpe Building
2101 N. Lincoln Boulevard
Oklahoma City, OK 73105

State Arts Council
Peter Hero
835 Summer Street, N.E.
Salem, OR 97301

State Arts Council
Peter Carnahan
3 Shore Drive
Office Center, 2001
N. Front Street
Harrisburg, PA 17102

State Arts Council
Robin Berry
334 Westminster Mall
Providence, RI 02903

State Arts Council
Rich George
1800 Gervaes Street
Columbia, SC 29201

South Dakota Arts Council
108 West 11th
Sioux Falls, SD 57102

State Arts Council
Arthur L. Keeble
222 Capital Hall Building
Nashville, TN 37219

Council of the Arts
Allen Longacre
P.O. Box 1346, Capital Station
Austin, TX 78711

Utah Arts Council
Arley G. Curtz
617 East South Temple Street
Salt Lake City, UT 84102

State Arts Council
Ellen McCulloch-Lovell
136 State Street
Montpelier, VT 05602

State Arts Council
Jerry Haynie
400 E. Grace Street, 1st Fl.
Richmond, VA 23219

State Arts Council
James L. Haseltine
9th and Columbia Building
Mail Stop FU-12
Olympia, WA 98504

State Arts Council
West Virginia Dept. of Culture and
   History
Capitol Complex
Charleston, WV 25305

State Arts Council
Jerrold Rouby
123 W. Washington Avenue
Madison, WI 53702

State Arts Council
John Bukler
122 West 25th Street
Cheyenne, WY 82002

Sunshine Artists, a monthly
publication originating in Winterpark, Florida, is probably the
most invaluable periodical for
anyone interested in attending
crafts fairs. Annual recognized
events total well over 1,100. You
can write to them for subscription
information at:

Sunshine Artists
Sun Country Enterprises
501—503 North Virginia Avenue
Winterpark, FL 32789
(305) 645-3155

American Craft is a bi-monthly
magazine with articles and photo-
graphs focusing on various crafts,
both old and new, and the artists
behind them. The back of each is-
sue features a state-by-state
breakdown of timely fairs and
events. You can also find information on shop galleries, workshops,
even recognized schools with
crafts courses. And for the craftsmaster, ideas and listings of
places to show your work. For
more information on how to receive *American Craft* write:

American Craft
Membership Dept.
American Craft Council
P.O. Box 561
Martinsville, NJ 08836

Photography: David Frazier, Nick Gunderson, David Leach, Toby Richards, Janis Tracy-Andrus

Additional Photography: Jon Elliot, Michael Kanouff, Majorie Ryerson, Jeffrey Weiss

COUNTRY PROPERTY Photography: William Robinson

NATURAL GARDEN Text and Photography: Ken Druse

Acknowledgements: Barry Bishop, Ronald and Victoria Borus, Jack and JoAnne Conti, Laura Cadwallader, Karen Day Hudson, Innocenti and Webel, *Greenvale*, *New Jersey*, Sybil Ittman, Leaming's Run Botanical Garden, *Swainton*, *Cape May County*, *New Jersey*, Joan Lyons, Sidney and Miriam Perle, Stuart and Maryann Teacher, Mr. and Mrs. John L. Thompson, Irene Wilkert, Anna and Magruder Wingfield

Thanks to the following people for allowing us to photograph their homes for this book: Jim and Aku Lawrence, Fran and David McCullough, Bob and Marilyn Muessel, Dan and Carol Raycraft, Lucy and Bill Sullivan, Jane and David Walentas

Special thanks to Ward Mohrfeld, Suzanne Slesin, Karen Graul, Walter Berkower, and The Museum of American Folk Crafts